FACTS ABOUT IRELAND

Published by the Department of Foreign Affairs, Dublin, Ireland
Design and artwork by Bill and Tina Murphy
Graphs by Paul Francis
Index compiled by Helen Litton

Colour origination by Pentacolour Ltd
Printed in Ireland by ßetaprint

Dublin 1995

Editorial date: April, 1995

ISBN 0 906404 23 1

CONTENTS

The object of this book is to give a general overview of the political, economic, social and cultural life of Ireland, its history and governmental structure. It is designed mainly for people abroad with an interest in Ireland. While the material in the book is intended to cover the most important areas of Irish life, it is not possible in the short space available to include everything. The short bibliography given at the end indicates where more complete treatment of the various subject-areas may be found. Current economic and budgetary data, where given, are in most cases provisional in nature.

Except where otherwise indicated, the material in this book relates to the Republic of Ireland.

Each of the seven chapters of this edition is introduced by a map featuring Ireland. There is a also a route map at the end of the book. The following are brief notes on the maps:

Note on the maps

Chapter 1, Land and People, page 1:
The map of Europe was produced from multiple photos taken by the AVHRR ('advanced very high resolution radiometer') satellite. The final image was constructed by ERA-Maptec using the computer facilities at Trinity College, Dublin.

Chapter 2, The Irish State, page 31:
The map of Ireland and Britain is from the *Geography* of Claudius Ptolemy which was compiled in Alexandria in the second century AD. This version was composed at Constantinople from the coordinates listed in the *Geography*. It is generally attributed to the twelfth century but is possibly much older. Ptolemy's map is remarkable for the accuracy of its general outline and for its detail. Names are attached, in Greek, to some sixty features in Ireland, and a number of rivers, kingdoms and royal centres can be identified with certainty. The original of the map is in the Vatican Library.

Chapter 3, Northern Ireland, page 61:
John Speed's map was published in London in 1612 as part of his *Theatre of the empire of Great Britaine*. The map includes geographical detail which became available to the cartographer for the first time following the conquest of Ulster. The map is in the Neptune Gallery, Dublin.

Chapter 4, Ireland in the World, page 73:
The map of Europe ca. AD 1200 is from Giraldus Cambrensis' *Topographia Hiberniae*. Cambrensis (meaning 'the Welshman') visited Ireland twice in the decade following the Norman invasion. The map may have been intended as a guide for travellers to Rome. The detail on Ireland relates primarily to the south-eastern part of the country which was the main sphere of Norman influence at the end of the twelfth century. The map is in the National Library of Ireland.

Chapter 5, The Economy, page 87:
The satellite map of Ireland was produced from ten separate photos taken by the Landsat 1 satellite at an altitude of 900 kms above the earth. The final image was constructed by ERA-Maptec at Trinity College, Dublin.

Chapter 6, Services, page 119:
The geological map was produced by the Geological Survey of Ireland. It illustrates also a cross-section of the country's geology from the north-west to the south-east.

Chapter 7, Culture, page 137:
The child's impression of Ireland is a hand-painting by Ms. Sarah Keenan, a National School pupil at Swords, Co. Dublin.

Route map, page 189:
This was produced on a digital database by the Ordnance Survey of Ireland.

1. Satellite Map of Europe

IRELAND

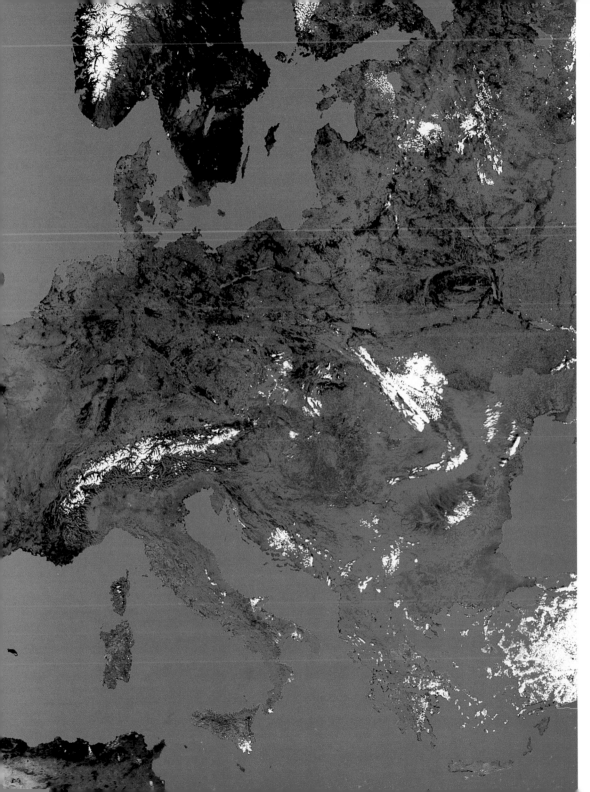

Physical Features

The island of Ireland is situated in the extreme north-west of Europe between $51\frac{1}{2}°$ and $55\frac{1}{2}°$ north latitude and between $5\frac{1}{2}°$ and $10\frac{1}{2}°$ west longitude.

The Irish Sea to the east, which separates Ireland from Britain, is from 17.6 to 192 km (11 to 120 miles) wide and has a maximum depth of about 200 metres (650 feet). Around the other coasts the shallow waters of the Continental Shelf are rather narrow and depths increase rapidly into the Atlantic Ocean.

Total Area	84,421 sq. km (32,595 sq. miles)
Republic of Ireland	70,282 sq. km (27,136 sq. miles)
Northern Ireland	14,139 sq. km (5,459 sq. miles)
Greatest length (N–S)	486 km (302 miles)
Greatest width (E–W)	275 km (171 miles)
Total coastline	5,631 km (3,500 miles)

*Facing page:
2. Trinity College, Dublin in winter. Ireland's climate is equable, and snow is unusual on the low-lying areas of the East coast.*

The island comprises a large central lowland of limestone with a relief of hills surrounded by a discontinuous border of coastal mountains which vary greatly in geological structure. The mountain ridges of the south are composed of old red sandstone separated by limestone river valleys. Granite predominates in the mountains of Galway, Mayo and Donegal in the west and north-west and in Counties Down and Wicklow on the east coast, while a basalt plateau covers much of the north-east of the country. The central plain, which is broken in places by low hills, is extensively covered with glacial deposits of clay and sand. It has considerable areas of bog and numerous lakes.

The island has seen at least two general glaciations and everywhere ice-smoothed rock, mountain lakes, glacial valleys and deposits of glacial sand, gravel and clay mark the passage of the ice.

Influenced by the Gulf Stream and with the prevailing winds predominantly from the south-west, the climate is equable and temperatures are fairly uniform over the whole country. The coldest months are January and February with mean daily

air temperatures of between 4°C and 7°C, while July and August are the warmest (14°C to 16°C). May and June are the sunniest months, averaging 5 to 7 hours of sunshine per day. In low-lying areas average annual rainfall is mostly between 800 and 1200mm (31" to 47") but ranges from less than 750mm (30") in some eastern areas to 1500mm (59") in parts of the west. In mountainous areas annual rainfall may exceed 2000mm (79").

Ireland was separated from the European mainland in the period following the last Ice Age. As a result the island has a smaller range of flora and fauna than is found elsewhere in Europe.

Climate

3. The Burren, Co. Clare.

Wildlife

4. Saint Dabeoc's Heath (Daboecia cantabrica), Connemara.

5. A stag from the national herd of red deer (Cervus elephus), Glenveagh National Park.

Much of the country was once covered with primeval forest. Although the original forests have been cleared over most of the country, remnants of the old natural forest in the Killarney area indicate that oak interspersed with holly and birch predominated, with ash, hazel and yew forests occurring in limestone areas.

These forests were very rich in lichens, mosses, liverworts and ferns. In recent decades the re-afforestation programme has favoured Sitka spruce, Scots, contorta and

6. The Jewel Anemone (Corynactis viridis) lives beneath over-hanging rocks along the southern and western coasts.

other pines, larches, Norway spruce and Douglas fir.

Raised peat bogs, varying in size from a couple of hectares to a few square kilometres, occur in the Central Plain in areas of impeded drainage while mountain bogs are common in western areas with heavy rainfall. The flora of the bogs consists of a large variety of bog-moss species together with heather and sedges. Two especially interesting botanical areas are Glengariff and Killarney (Cork/Kerry) which are very rich in bryophytes and lichen species of extreme oceanic and even tropical distribution. The Burren in Co. Clare is a region of bare carboniferous limestone, containing arctic-alpine species surviving from the last glaciation and Mediterranean species at the northern end of their range.

Rivers and lakes contain a wide variety of fish life. Salmon, trout, char, pollan and eel all occur naturally and other varieties, such as pike, roach and rainbow trout, have been introduced from outside. The only amphibians are a single species each of frog, toad and newt. There are no snakes and the only reptile is the common lizard.

Of some 380 species of wild birds recorded in Ireland, 135 breed in the country. There is considerable migration of birds to Ireland in spring and autumn, while winter migration brings a number of species from Greenland and Iceland. Three-quarters of the world population of the Greenland whitefronted goose winter in Ireland. The significance of this has been marked by the establishment of an internationally important wildlife reserve in Co. Wexford. There is also considerable passage migration from the south by birds which nest further north.

7. The Spring Gentian (Gentiana verna) is native to Ireland and is especially abundant in the Burren.

8. Kingfisher (Alcedo atthis), breeds in every part of Ireland.

9. Bogland flowers.

Game shooting is strictly controlled and, in addition, there is a national network of refuges where all game shooting is prohibited. Some wild game bird stocks — mainly pheasant and mallard duck — are augmented through State-assisted restocking programmes. Inland waters support colonies of swans, geese, waders, duck, tern and gulls.

Mammals are similar to those found throughout the temperate regions of Europe. Of the 31 species which occur, the Irish stoat and the Irish hare are the most interesting examples of native development. Other animals include the fox, badger, rabbit, otter, squirrel and hedgehog.

The *National Parks and Wildlife Service* of The Office of Public Works is responsible for conservation in the Republic of Ireland. Most species of wild fauna and several species of wild flora are protected. Conservation of wildlife habitats is achieved through the creation of nature reserves of which there are 75, together with 5 refuges for fauna.

In recent years State forests have been opened to the public. There are now 12 large forest parks and over 400 smaller amenities. Public access is generally limited to pedestrians and these centres offer excellent opportunities for observing wildlife in its natural surroundings.

The National Parks and Wildlife Service is also responsible for the development and management of national parks and nature reserves.

To date, five national parks have been established. All five meet international standards for national parks, conserving as they do outstanding parts of the natural heritage. They are located at Killarney,

10. *Heritage sites managed by the Office of Public Works.*

NATIONAL MONUMENT
NATIONAL PARK
NATIONAL HISTORIC PROPERTY
NATURE RESERVE
OTHER PROPERTIES

Co. Kerry; Glenveagh, Co. Donegal; Connemara, Co. Galway; The Burren, Co. Clare; and the Wicklow Mountains, Co. Wicklow.

Environment

The economy has traditionally been based on agriculture and up to the 1960's the population lived largely in rural areas. Since then, the natural environment has been affected by policies to promote the establishment and expansion of modern industry, by a major enlargement of urban development, and by changed patterns of agriculture, including more intensive production. Despite increased pressures on the environment, late industrialisation and the predominance of clean modern industry have had the advantage of enabling major damage to be prevented or controlled.

Ireland's location off the west coast of Europe, with high annual rainfall and prevailing south-west winds from the Atlantic, contributes to the quality of the environment. The country is largely free from air pollution and its watercourses are of a very high standard. The low population density over much of the country has further helped to preserve the integrity of the landscape.

The protection of the environment is a major objective of Government. In addition to its intrinsic value and contribution to the quality of life, a clean environment is recognised as a crucial economic factor. It is of particular importance in the development of tourism, agriculture and food production, mariculture, aquaculture and other natural resource-based industries, and in the marketing abroad of quality products and services.

11. Glendalough, Co. Wicklow. A monastic site founded by St. Kevin in the sixth century, Glendalough went into decline following attacks by the Vikings.

12. Ireland's only commercially operated windmill, at Blennerville, Co. Kerry.

Legislation to protect and maintain the quality of the environment is implemented by local authorities and by the *Environmental Protection Agency*. The Agency promotes and implements standards for environmental protection and management. From 1994 it has been responsible for licensing those categories of development which have the greatest potential to cause pollution.

Population

Ireland has been inhabited since Stone Age times. For more than five thousand years peoples moving westwards across the European continent have settled in the country and each new group of immigrants, Celts, Vikings, Normans, English, has contributed to its present population. In 1841, shortly before the Great Famine, the area comprising the present Irish State had a population of over 6.5 million. The next census (1851) showed a massive decline to 5.1 million for the same area, due to deaths from starvation and disease and large-scale emigration.

The outflow thus begun became a dominant feature of the population pattern over the succeeding years. By 1961 the population of the State stood at 2.8 million, the lowest census figure on record. From 1961 onwards the pattern changed. A combination of natural increase and the commencement of inward net migration resulting from increased prosperity produced an average annual rise in population of 0.6% in the period 1981 to 1986. Between 1986 and 1991, largely as a result of the resumption of emigration, an average annual fall in population of 0.1% was recorded. At the 1991 census the total population of the State was 3,525,719. In 1994 the population was estimated at 3.571 million.

The major centres of population are Dublin (915,000), Cork (174,000), Limerick (75,000), Galway (51,000), Waterford (42,000), and Dundalk (30,000). 59% of the population live in cities and towns of 1,000 people or more. Overall population density is 51 persons per square kilometre with large variations between the east and south, where densities are highest, and the less populous west of the country.

A high proportion of the population is concentrated in the younger age-groups. Approximately 43% of the population is under 25 and approximately 27% is under 15.

In 1993 for the first time on record the birth rate fell below the minimum population

Figure 1.1

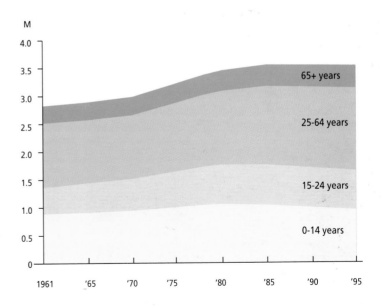

Population 1961–1995

replacement rate of 2.1 births per woman during child-rearing age, to 1.93 births per woman. Total births in 1993 were 49,456 and, if present trends continue, the annual number of births could fall below 40,000 by the year 2007. This compares with a peak of 74,064 births recorded in 1980.

Religion

Freedom of conscience and the free profession and practice of religion are, subject to public order and morality, Constitutionally guaranteed. The State guarantees not to endow any religion.

The majority of the people belong to Christian denominations. At the 1991 census, approximately 92% of the population of the Republic of Ireland were classified as Roman Catholic, approximately 3% as Protestant (including Church of Ireland: 2.35%; Presbyterian: 0.37%; Methodist: 0.14%). There is a small but long-established Jewish Community (0.04%). The remainder of the population belonged to other religious groups, many of them newly-established in Ireland (Islamic: 0.11%, Jehovah's Witnesses: 0.10%, etc.) or claimed no specific religious beliefs.

The main religious denominations are organised on an all-Ireland basis. They are as follows:

■ The Roman Catholic Church
The Catholic Church has four ecclesiastical provinces, each with its own archbishop: Armagh, Dublin, Cashel and Tuam, covering the north, east, south and west of the country, respectively. Each province consists of a number of dioceses, of which there are 27 in all. The Archbishop of Armagh is the Primate of All Ireland and is normally a Cardinal. The present diocesan structure has remained basically the same since the 12th century and does not conform to modern political divisions.

The combined Catholic population of the Republic and of Northern Ireland is about 3.9 million. There are approximately 1,300 parishes served by about 4,000 priests. The rate of religious practice among Irish Catholics is one of the highest in the world. There are approximately 20,000 men and women in various religious orders of priests, brothers and nuns.

The Catholic Church is closely involved in the provision of education and health services. This involvement began as a service to the poor but expanded considerably over the years. The Church cooperates with State agencies in many areas such as education and welfare.

The Irish Catholic Church sends missionaries to every continent. Today there are over 4,500 Irish missionaries working in 85 different countries throughout Africa, Asia, Central and South America, and Oceania.

■ The Church of Ireland
The Church of Ireland is a Protestant Episcopal Church, an autonomous church within the worldwide Anglican Communion. The Church is organised into twelve dioceses. The Archbishop of Armagh is the Primate of All Ireland and the only other Archbishopric is Dublin. Chief legislative power lies with the General Synod, consisting of the archbishops, bishops, 216 representatives of the clergy and 432 representatives of the laity. The clerical and lay representatives are elected every three

years. The Church of Ireland is actively involved in education and social services. The total membership of the Church of Ireland is around 380,000, 75% of whom live in Northern Ireland.

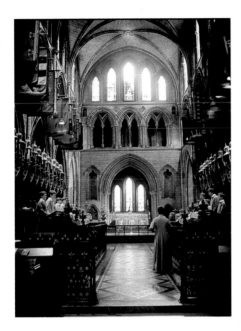

13. St. Patrick's, Dublin, is the national cathedral of the Church of Ireland. Built in the 13th Century by the Normans, St Patrick's today is often the venue for ecumenical services of the Christian churches.

■ The Presbyterian Church

The Presbyterian Church is a Protestant Church of the Reformed tradition with a strong emphasis on the authority of the Scriptures in the life of the Christian. The Church has 558 congregations or parishes grouped into 21 districts called Presbyteries, and five regional Synods. These are all represented at the highest court of the Church, known as the General Assembly of ministers and elders. Elders are men and women elected by the congregation and are responsible for the spiritual welfare of Church members. The Assembly makes rules and decides the policies of the Church. It meets annually and is presided over by the

Moderator who is elected to represent the Presbyterian Church for a one year period. The Presbyterian Church in Ireland has ordained women to the ministry since the 1950's. There are approximately 312,000 Presbyterians in Ireland, more than 95% of whom live in Northern Ireland. Most of the latter stem from the 17th century Plantation of Ulster.

■ The Methodist Church

The Methodist Church in Ireland owes its origins to the missions of John Wesley, the evangelic preacher who visited the country on several occasions in the 18th century. Although closely linked to British Methodism, the Irish Methodist Church is an autonomous body with its own President and Secretary. There are 240 local churches grouped into 77 Circuits which are in turn grouped into eight Districts. The Methodist Church has approximately 130 ministers engaged in active parish duties. The total membership of the Church in Ireland is around 60,000 people, about 90% of whom live in Northern Ireland.

Irish Methodism has developed a wide range of social work activities, mainly through its missions in the larger cities. These provide facilities for the elderly and the needy. The Church is also involved in education.

Article 8 of the Constitution makes the following affirmation:

1. *The Irish language as the national language is the first official language.*
2. *The English language is recognized as a second official language.*

Language

History of the Irish Language

Irish is a Celtic language and, as such, is a member of the Indo-European family of languages. Within the Celtic group, it belongs to the Goidelic branch of insular Celtic. Irish has evolved from a form of Celtic which was introduced into Ireland at some period during the great Celtic migrations of antiquity between the end of the second millennium and the fourth century BC. Old Irish, Ireland's vernacular when the historical period begins in the sixth century of our era, is the earliest variant of the Celtic languages, and indeed the earliest of European vernaculars north of the Alps, in which extensive writings are extant.

The Norse settlements (AD 800 onwards) and the Anglo-Norman colonization (AD 1169 onwards) introduced periods of new language diversity into Ireland, but Irish remained dominant and other speech communities were gradually assimilated. In the early sixteenth century, almost all of the population was Irish-speaking. The main towns, however, prescribed English for the formal conduct of administrative and legal business.

The events of the later sixteenth century and of the seventeenth century for the first time undermined the status of Irish as a major language. The Tudor and Stuart conquests and plantations (1534–1610), the Cromwellian settlement (1654), and the Williamite war (1689–91) followed by the enactment of the Penal Laws (1695), had the cumulative effect of eliminating the Irish-speaking ruling classes and of destroying their cultural institutions. They were replaced by a new ruling class, or Ascendancy, whose language was English, and thereafter English was the sole language of government and public institutions. Irish continued as the language of the greater part of the rural population and, for a time, of the servant classes in towns.

From the middle of the eighteenth century, as the Penal Laws were relaxed and a greater social and economic mobility became possible for the native Irish, the more prosperous of the Irish-speaking community

14. Irish/Latin/English phrasebook compiled for Queen Elizabeth of England (16th Century).

15. *The Aran Islands, Co. Galway; part of the Gaeltacht.*

began to conform to the prevailing middle-class ethos by adopting English. Irish thus began to be associated with poverty and economic deprivation. This tendency increased after the Act of Union in 1800.

Yet because of the rapid growth of the rural population, the actual number of Irish speakers increased substantially during the first decades of the nineteenth century. In 1835 their number was estimated at four million. This number consisted almost entirely of an impoverished rural population which was decimated by the Great Famine and by resultant mass emigration. By 1891,

the number of Irish speakers had been reduced to 680,000 and, according to that year's census of population, Irish speakers under the age of ten represented no more than 3.5% of their age-group.

When the position began to stabilize early in the twentieth century, Irish remained as a community language only in small discontinuous regions, mainly around the western seaboard. These regions are collectively called the *Gaeltacht*. In the 1991 census, the population of the officially-defined Gaeltacht aged three years and over was 79,563, of whom 56,469 or 71% were returned as Irish-speaking. The number of Irish speakers is a decreasing proportion of the total because, for a variety of complex reasons, some of the indigenous population of the Gaeltacht continue to shift to English, and because new English-speaking households are settling there.

On the other hand, there are many Irish-speaking individuals and families throughout the rest of the country, particularly in Dublin.

16. Key to Ogham in the Book of Ballymote, 14th and 15th Centuries.

Below:
17. Pillarstone with Ogham inscriptions, Coolnagort, Dunloe, Co. Kerry.

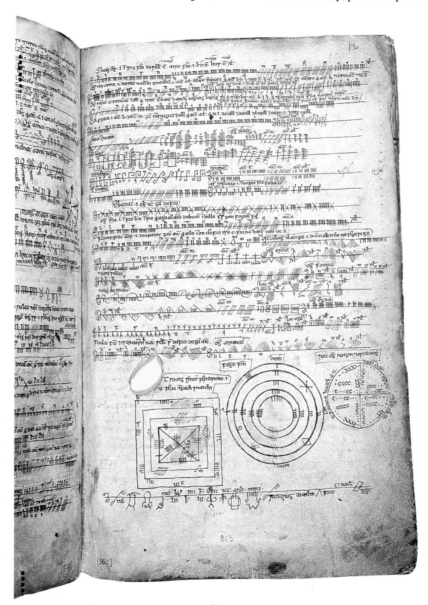

In 1991 just under 1.1 million people or 32.5% of the total population aged three years or over, were returned as Irish-speaking, but this figure does not distinguish differing degrees of competence and use.

Towards the end of the eighteenth century the Anglo-Irish Ascendancy had begun to develop an academic interest in the Irish language and its literature. Academic interest later merged with a concern for the survival of spoken Irish as its decline became increasingly evident. Language-related activity grew throughout the nineteenth century and, following the establishment in 1893 of the Gaelic League, or in Irish *Conradh na Gaeilge*, the objective of maintaining and extending the use of Irish as a vernacular fused with the renewed separatist movement which culminated in the establishment of the Irish Free State in 1922.

The State has made various provisions for the maintenance and promotion of the language. Irish is an obligatory subject at primary and second level schools. The Department of Arts, Culture and the Gaeltacht has responsibility for promoting the cultural, social, and economic welfare of the Gaeltacht, and more generally for encouraging the use of Irish as a vernacular. The Department has two statutory boards

18. *Books in Irish.*

under its aegis: *Údarás na Gaeltachta* 'Gaeltacht Authority', some of whose members are elected by the people of the Gaeltacht, is a development authority for Gaeltacht areas; *Bord na Gaeilge* 'Irish-language board' has responsibility for the promotion of Irish as a vernacular throughout the country.

■ *Varieties of Irish*

The earliest known form of Irish is preserved in Ogham (Old Irish spelling *ogam*) inscriptions which date mainly from the fourth and fifth centuries of our era. The linguistic information preserved in Ogham is sparse, as the inscriptions contain little more than personal names, but it is sufficient to reveal a form of Goidelic much older than Old Irish, the earliest well-documented variety of the language.

Old Irish was the language of Ireland's 'Golden Age', and its classical phase is generally assigned to the period AD 700–850. Old Irish evolved into Middle Irish, the language of the late Viking and post-Viking period. In comparison with Old Irish, Middle Irish is characterized by a simplification of the inflections of noun and verb and of the system of pronouns.

By 1200 Early Modern Irish, or Classical Modern Irish, had begun to emerge. This is the language of the period of Gaelic resurgence when Old Irish, Norse, Norman, and Old English were largely assimilated into a new Irish-speaking society. This form of Irish lasted from the thirteenth century to the seventeenth as the literary norm for the whole Gaelic world, which comprised Ireland, Gaelic Scotland, and the Isle of Man. During the seventeenth century, as the influence of

ᴀbcᴅeꝼᵹ ıꝇmnopꞃꞅꞇu

the old literary schools and learned classes receded, the forms of the written language became increasingly regional in character. In this period the autonomous forms of Modern Irish, Scots Gaelic, and Manx became established. Even so, at the end of the nineteenth century and the beginning of the twentieth, as the Irish revival gathered momentum, there were many who felt that Classical Modern Irish was still the most appropriate norm for literary purposes. Since the advocates of this view not only used the older grammatical forms, but imitated the ornate and sometimes ponderous style of Early Modern prose, they brought a reaction from writers such as Peadar Ó Laoghaire, Pádraic Ó Conaire, and Patrick Pearse, who were developing a literary diction based on contemporary speech.

The 'speech of the people' movement triumphed, but one, perhaps unforeseen, result was that the written language for a time became quite diversified, as writers went their divergent ways in representing contemporary usage. It was necessary to redefine norms. A new spelling norm was published in 1945 and, in emended form, in 1947; a new grammatical norm was published in 1953 and, in revised form, in 1958. These are now codified in Ó Dónaill's official Irish-English dictionary, *Foclóir Gaeilge-Béarla*, which appeared in 1978.

■ *The English Language in Ireland*
The Anglo-Norman aristocracy who established themselves in Ireland after 1169 spoke a variety of French, but they brought in their train, as retainers and traders, a substantial community of English-speakers. English has been spoken continuously in Ireland since that time. It is now the first language of the majority of the population, and most native speakers of Irish speak it fluently as a second language.

From the thirteenth century to the seventeenth, however, the Irish-speaking community was strongly assimilative of other groups. In the early sixteenth century, the number of monoglot English-speakers who were of Irish birth must have been extremely small. One obvious consequence of this fact is the absence of any long-established Irish dialects of English. Indeed, some phonological features of Irish English show clearly that it began first to be adopted as the vernacular in the later eighteenth century.

The more unusual features of Irish English are largely due to influence from the Irish which it replaced. Such influence is found in the phonetics of many rural varieties of Irish English. But the first generations who adopted English were influenced by Irish in their vocabulary, grammar, and idiom as well as in their pronunciation. Their speech was used as a basis for a literary diction by J.M. Synge (1871–1909), Douglas Hyde (1860–1949), and by other writers of their generation. But this speech was a transitional form and its more distinctive features have now almost completely disappeared.

Today, Irish English is increasingly an unremarkable variant of General English. Like American English, though, it continues to show a degree of autonomy which is the more surprising when one considers the country's physical and communicative proximity to Great Britain.

History

■ *Prehistory*

The earliest settlers arrived around 7,000 BC in the mesolithic or middle stone-age period. They arrived in the north across the narrow strait from Britain. These people were mainly hunters.

Colonists of the neolithic, or new stone-age, period reached Ireland around 3,000 BC. These were farmers who raised animals and cultivated the soil. Many remnants of their civilization — houses, pottery, implements — have been excavated at Lough Gur in Co. Limerick and some can be seen at the folk park now developed around the lakeside site. The neolithic colonists were largely self-sufficient but engaged in a limited form of trading in products such as axe-heads.

Many of their religious monuments have survived, the most impressive of which is the great megalithic tomb at Newgrange in Co. Meath.

Prospectors and metalworkers arrived about 2,000 BC. Metal deposits were discovered and soon bronze and gold objects were being manufactured. Many artifacts made by these bronze-age people have been found, among them axe-heads, pottery and jewellery. About 1,200 BC another movement of people reached Ireland, producing an even greater variety of weapons and artifacts. A common type of dwelling in use at this time was the *crannóg*, an artificial island, pallisaded on all sides, constructed in the middle of a lake.

The people who made the greatest impact on Ireland were the Celts. The earliest waves of Celtic invaders may have reached the country from central Europe as early as the 6th century BC with subsequent groups arriving up to the time of Christ. The Celts belonged linguistically to the great Indo-European family. They soon came to dominate Ireland and the earlier settlers.

The Celtic culture of the La Tène civilization — named after a Celtic site in Switzerland — reached Ireland around the 2nd century BC.

Celtic Ireland was not unified politically,

20. Newgrange, Co. Meath, a megalithic passage grave which dates from about 3,000 B.C. A small opening in the stonework is designed to admit sunlight to illuminate the central point of the burial chamber at dawn, during winter solstice.

21. The Ardagh Chalice. Of polished silver and gilt bronze panels, the Chalice is the finest expression of 8th Century Irish metal working.

only by culture and language. The country was divided into about 150 miniature kingdoms, each called a *tuath*. A minor king ruled a *tuath*, subject to a more powerful king who ruled a group of *tuatha*, who was in turn subject to one of the five provincial kings. This political situation was very fluid, with constant shifts in power among the most important contenders.

Celtic Ireland had a simple agrarian economy. No coins were used and the unit of exchange was the cow. People lived on individual farms and there were no towns. Society was rigidly stratified into classes and was regulated by the Brehon Laws, an elaborate code of legislation based largely on the concepts of the *tuath* as the political unit and the *fine*, or extended family, as the social unit.

■ *Early Christian Period*
Christianity was introduced in the 5th century. This is traditionally associated with St Patrick (d. 461) although there were some Christians in the country before his arrival. The first written documents date from this period. A distinctive feature of the development of early Irish Christianity was the important role played by monasticism. The great monasteries such as Glendalough, founded by St Kevin, and Clonmacnoise, founded by St Ciaran, were famous centres of culture and learning and the illuminated manuscripts which they produced were among the glories of Irish monasticism.

It was through the monasteries that Irish influence on Britain and Europe was exerted from the 6th century onwards. Setting out first as pilgrims, Irish monks preached the Gospel and established new communities across the continent. Ireland, unlike most of the rest of Europe, did not suffer barbarian invasion and so acted as a repository of Christian civilization at a time when it was almost extinguished elsewhere. Irish monks are associated with a number of continental

22. *The 8th Century Book of Kells, the finest illuminated manuscript from Ireland's 'Golden Age', now in the library of Trinity College, Dublin. The Book contains a text in Latin of the four gospels, with prefaces, summaries and canon tables. The illustration is of a canon table in the majuscule script.*

centres — St Fursey at Peronne in France, St Kilian at Wurzburg in Germany, St Vergil at Salzburg in Austria, St Columbanus at Bobbio in Italy. They brought Christianity to pagan peoples, established centres of learning and paved the way for the intellectual flowering in 9th century France known as the Carolingian Renaissance. One of the most notable of these monks was the philosopher and theologian Johannes Scotus Eriugena.

The successful missionary efforts of the Irish abroad were matched by rich cultural achievements at home. Elaborate chalices, croziers and ornamental jewellery were fashioned while the scribes committed the rich classical tradition to their magnificently illuminated manuscripts. This period from the 6th to the 9th century has been seen by many as the Golden Age of Irish history.

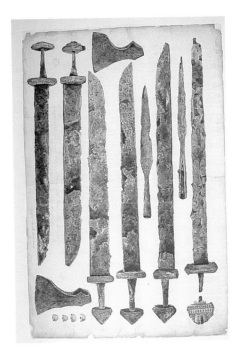

23. Weapons from the Viking burial ground at Kilmainham, Dublin (9th Century).

◼ *The Middle Ages*

From around 800 onwards Ireland was attacked by bands of Viking marauders. The raids continued right through the 9th century and a second major wave began early in the 10th century. The monasteries, as the major centres of population and wealth, were the main target of the Vikings. They were despoiled of their books and valuables and many of them were burned. These attacks, and attacks by the Irish themselves, contributed to the decline of the great monastic tradition at this period.

The Vikings were great traders and did much to develop commerce in medieval Ireland. They founded most of the major towns such as Dublin, Cork, Limerick and Waterford.

The lack of any political unity made it difficult to resist the Viking attacks.

However, the strength of the Uí Néill kings in the northern half of the country prevented the Vikings from establishing themselves there. Towards the end of the 10th century a new dynasty emerged in Munster in the south and, under the kingship of Brian Boru, was able to match the Uí Néill. Brian Boru defeated the Vikings in 999 and in 1002 he won recognition as king of all Ireland. The Vikings intervened regularly in the disputes between the Irish kings. Their support for a Leinster revolt against Brian Boru led to their defeat at the Battle of Clontarf in 1014, after which they were confined to a subsidiary role in Irish political history.

The 11th and 12th centuries were an age of renaissance and progress in Ireland. Cultural activity and the arts prospered. It was a great era of religious reform and a powerful effort was made to bring the church

24. *Diarmait Mac Murchada from Geraldus Cambrensis' 'Expugnatio Hibernica'.*

GERALDVS·FILIVS·GERALDI · COMES ·
KILDARIE·ÆTATIS·43·Ã·DÑĪ·1530·

25. *Garret Óg Fitzgerald, ninth Earl of Kildare, served as Lord Deputy for Ireland (1513-1534) in succession to his father. His fall from royal favour during the reign of King Henry VIII marked the begining of the end for Norman and Gaelic autonomy.*

more fully into line with Roman orthodoxy. Two of the principal figures of this movement were St Malachy of Armagh (d. 1148) and St Laurence O'Toole of Dublin (d. 1180). In politics, others sought to follow Brian Boru's example and establish themselves as kings of all Ireland. At various times between 1014 and 1169 the kings of Munster, Ulster, Connacht and Leinster succeeded in doing so. The general trend was towards the development of a strong centralised monarchy on the European model.

This trend was interrupted by the arrival of the Normans in 1167–69. The first Normans came to Ireland from south Wales at the invitation of Diarmait Mac Murchada, king of Leinster, to support his ambition to become king of all Ireland. Mac Murchada was succeeded as King of Leinster by the leader of the Normans, Richard de Clare,

known as Strongbow. In 1171 the Normans' overlord, Henry II, King of England, came to Ireland and was recognised as overlord of the country by both Irish and Normans. Thus began the political involvement of England in Ireland which was to dominate the country's history in succeeding centuries.

The Normans quickly came to control three-quarters of the land. In time, they assimilated with the local population until they became, it was said, more Irish than the Irish themselves. The Normans had a major impact on the country. Throughout the 13th century they developed the same type of parliament, law and system of administration as in England.

However, the native, or Gaelic, Irish exerted pressure on the Norman colony. Outside the colony attempts were made to re-establish the native kingship. Edward Bruce, brother of the Scottish king Robert, failed in his attempt in 1315, the last serious effort to overthrow Norman rule. By the end of the 15th century, due to the depredations of the Irish and the Gaelicisation of the leading Norman families, the area of English rule in Ireland had shrunk to a small enclave around Dublin known as the Pale.

◼ Early Modern Period

In the 16th century the Tudor monarchs began a reconquest of Ireland. Henry VIII declared himself king of Ireland in 1541, the first English monarch to do so. The Tudors introduced new English settlers and embarked on a series of military campaigns against the Gaelic Irish and the great Anglo-Norman lords who had fallen away in their allegiance to the Crown. When the army of Elizabeth defeated the Irish at the battle of Kinsale in 1601, it marked the beginning of a new order. The native political system was overthrown and for the first time the entire country was run by a strong English central Government.

From the 16th century onwards the English Government made strenuous efforts to impose Protestantism. The reformed religion did not really take root, however, partly due to its close association with the repressive policies of the English administration. The main exception was in Ulster where the Government promoted a successful colonization by new settlers, mostly Scottish Presbyterians.

Religion added complexity to the political situation. The new colonists were Protestant and formed a distinct group from the Old English, the remnants of the Anglo-Irish colony who were still Catholic and increasingly disaffected from the Government. To a large extent political power and office were now in the hands of the colonists, the New English. When the Gaelic Irish of Ulster rebelled against the Government in 1641 they were soon joined by their Old English co-religionists. In 1642 a rebel assembly, the **Confederation of Kilkenny**, met, but divisions soon appeared as Ireland became enmeshed in the English civil war between King and Parliament. The rebellion was ruthlessly crushed by Oliver Cromwell and his parliamentary army.

Further Protestant colonization took place under Cromwell. This time the large-scale confiscation of land and the banishment of its former owners to the poorer areas of the country ensured that property and political power passed to the new colonists. The accession of the Catholic King James II in 1685 changed the situation only temporarily. His pro-Catholic stance was unpopular in England and Scotland and among the Ulster Scots. When William of Orange challenged James II for the throne the entire country except Ulster backed James. The two kings contested their throne in Ireland and William emerged victorious after a series of battles, the most famous being William's defeat of James at the Boyne in 1690. William's victory left the Irish Catholics politically helpless and made possible the Protestant ascendancy that followed. Many leading Catholics like Patrick Sarsfield (James' commander-in-chief) went abroad to serve in continental armies.

◼ 18th Century

Throughout the 18th century Catholics were seen as a threat who might rally in support of a Stuart attempt to regain the English throne.

26. 'William III at the Battle of the Boyne', (Benjamin West).

27. 'The Irish House of Commons, 1780', (Francis Wheatley).

The Government enforced a severe code of penal legislation against them. The Presbyterians also suffered religious disabilities but on a much lesser scale. Power was concentrated in the hands of the small Protestant ascendancy.

The American War of Independence had an important influence on Irish politics. The American example encouraged the Protestant ascendancy to press for a measure of colonial self-government. In 1782 the Irish parliament, hitherto subservient to London, was granted independence. Ireland was now effectively a separate kingdom sharing a monarch with England, but the Dublin administration was still appointed by the King. One of the leading figures in this parliament was Henry Grattan. From 1778 onwards the penal legislation against Catholics was gradually repealed. The parliament made moves to improve and liberalise trade.

The French Revolution, with its ideas of equality and liberty, had a major impact on Ireland. **The Society of the United Irishmen** was founded in 1791 to press for radical reform. Its members were mainly Presbyterians from the north. The leading figures were Wolfe Tone, Napper Tandy and Lord Edward Fitzgerald. The war with France led to severe military repression in Ireland. The United Irishmen rebelled in 1798, aiming to unite Catholics and Protestants, including Presbyterians, and to break Ireland's link with England. In spite of French help the rebellion was badly organised and easily suppressed.

After the defeat of the rebellion, the London Government decided to unite the British and Irish parliaments. The Irish parliament, an unrepresentative assembly, was induced to vote itself out of existence in 1800.

■ *Modern Ireland*

From 1801 onwards Ireland had no Parliament of its own; Irish MPs (drawn from the ascendancy) sat in the Westminster parliament in London where they were a small minority. Westminster was unwilling to grant major concessions to Catholics, despite persistent agitation. In 1823 a Catholic barrister, Daniel O'Connell, established the **Catholic Association** to press for full liberty for Catholics and rapidly converted it into a political mass-movement. O'Connell's success forced the London parliament to grant Catholic Emancipation in 1829, removing virtually all the disabilities against Catholics.

O'Connell, the most popular figure in the country, now sought repeal of the Act of Union of 1800 and the restoration of the Irish parliament. He set up the **Repeal Association** and modelled his campaign on that for emancipation. The agitation was characterised by mass meetings, some attracting hundreds of thousands of people. The London Government resisted and when a Dublin rally was banned in 1843, O'Connell acquiesced. This marked the effective end of the repeal campaign.

In the 1840's the **Young Ireland** movement was formed. The most influential of its leaders was Thomas Davis who, like the United Irishmen, expressed a concept of nationality embracing all who lived in Ireland, regardless of creed or origin. An attempt by the Young Irelanders to stage an insurrection failed in 1848, but their ideas

28. 'O'Connell and His Contemporaries; the Clare election, 1828' (Joseph Haverty)

29. The Land War: Burning of the Duke of Leinster's leases at a meeting in Kildare (Illustrated London News, 8 January, 1881).

30. Memorial to the victims of the Famine, (Edward Delaney), St. Stephen's Green, Dublin.

strongly influenced later generations.

The end of war in Europe in 1815 had a drastic impact on the economy. The war had led to a huge growth in tillage farming to supply the armies, and a dependence on the potato as a staple food. When war ended there was a change from tillage to pasture, causing agrarian unemployment. Population increased rapidly and reached 8 million by 1841, two-thirds of whom depended on agriculture. In this precarious agrarian economy the failure of the potato crop in 1845, due to blight, proved disastrous. The crop failed again in 1846, 1847 and 1848 and, coupled with severe weather, resulted in famine. By 1851 the population had been reduced by at least 2 million due to starvation, disease and emigration to Britain and North America.

The latter half of the 19th century was characterised by campaigns for national independence and land reform. The **Irish Republican Brotherhood (IRB)**, also known as the Fenians, was founded in 1858. The Fenians, a secret society, rejected constitutional attempts to gain independence as futile. Among the leaders of the Fenians were James Stephens and John O'Leary. The Fenians staged an armed uprising in 1867. The rising was no more than a token gesture and was easily put down. The IRB continued in existence, however.

A constitutional movement seeking **Home Rule** was set up by Isaac Butt. The Home Rulers, who sought a separate parliament subordinate to London, won half the Irish seats in the 1874 election. Leadership of the movement soon passed to Charles Stewart Parnell.

The strained relations between landlords and their tenant farmers were a constant social and political difficulty. In 1879 Michael Davitt founded the **National Land League**. The League aimed to secure basic rights for tenant-farmers — fair rent, free sale and fixity of tenure. Parnell became president of the movement. Many Fenians also joined. The result was a great national campaign of mass agitation from 1879 to 1882 which forced the British Government to pass a series of Land Acts. These eventually abolished the old landlord system and transferred ownership of the land to the people who worked it.

Parnell then used the agrarian movement as the basis to agitate for Home Rule in the 1885 election. The Home Rule party swept the country outside eastern Ulster. Gladstone, the British Prime Minister, responded by introducing a Bill in Parliament to grant Home Rule but this was defeated in 1886, as was another in 1894. The impetus of the Home Rule campaign was effectively lost with the death of Parnell in 1891.

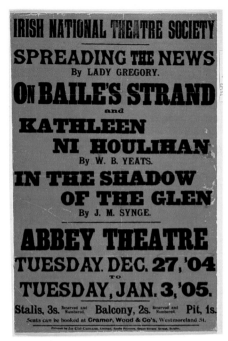

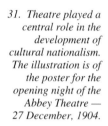

31. Theatre played a central role in the development of cultural nationalism. The illustration is of the poster for the opening night of the Abbey Theatre — 27 December, 1904.

However, the years after Parnell's death saw the growing emergence of a cultural nationalism. The **Gaelic Athletic Association**, founded in 1884, promoted the national games while the **Gaelic League**, founded in 1893 by Douglas Hyde and Eoin MacNeill, tried to revive the Irish language and culture on a nationwide basis. At the same time Arthur Griffith developed a new political party in the period 1905–08 known as **Sinn Féin** — 'we ourselves'. The **Sinn Féin** policy was that Irish MPs should withdraw from Westminster and establish an independent parliament. **Sinn Féin** had close links with the IRB. The Dublin labour dispute of 1913 produced another group, the **Irish Citizen Army**, which was socialist but also separatist.

In 1912 another Home Rule bill was introduced in Westminster. This brought considerable success to the **Irish Parliamentary Party**, now led by John Redmond. However, resistance to the measure was strong in north-east Ulster. It was led by Sir Edward Carson who set up the **Ulster Volunteers** to oppose Home Rule. In response, the **Irish Volunteers**, largely controlled by the IRB, were founded in Dublin.

The Home Rule bill was finally passed in 1914, but its implementation was shelved upon the outbreak of war. John Redmond encouraged Irishmen to enlist in the British Army hoping this would sustain British support for Home Rule. Others disagreed with this policy and in 1916 the **Irish Volunteers**, led by Patrick Pearse and the **Irish Citizen Army** led by James Connolly, staged a rebellion against British rule. The Easter Rising of 1916 was put down but the decision of the British to execute several of the leaders alienated public opinion. In the 1918 general election **Sinn Féin** totally defeated the Irish Parliamentary Party.

The **Sinn Féin** representatives now constituted themselves as the first **Dáil**, or independent Parliament, in Dublin. The **Dáil** was headed by Éamon de Valera. The British attempt to smash **Sinn Féin** led to the War of Independence of 1919–21. The Irish forces were led by Michael Collins. After more than two years of guerilla struggle a truce was agreed. In December 1921 an Anglo-Irish Treaty was signed and 26 counties gained independence as the **Irish Free State**. Six Ulster counties had been granted their own parliament in Belfast in 1920 and remained within the United Kingdom.

The establishment of the Free State was followed by a civil war between the new

32. *The Irish Citizen Army, 1916.*

33. *'The Birth of the Republic' (Walter Paget) depicts the scene within the General Post Office towards the end of the Easter Rising, 1916.*

Government and those who opposed the Treaty. Éamon de Valera led those who opposed the treaty. A truce was negotiated in May 1923 but the Civil War claimed the lives of many who had been prominent in the struggle for independence, among them Michael Collins and Cathal Brugha.

34. *Sinn Féin leaders at the first Dáil in 1919: Michael Collins (front row, 2nd left), Arthur Griffith (4th left), Éamon de Valera (5th left).*

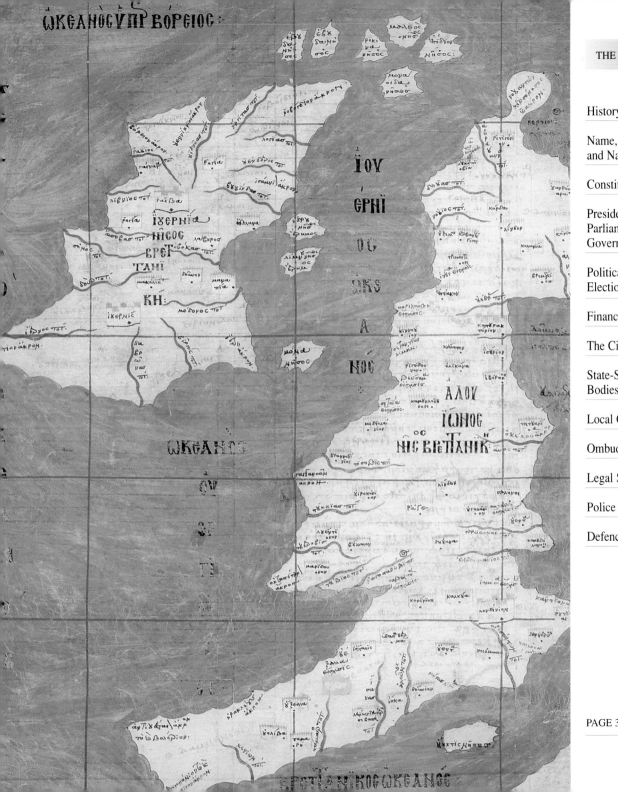

Preceding page:
35. Map of Ireland
('Iouernia') from the
Geography of
Claudius Ptolmey of
Alexandria
(ca. AD 150).

This page:
36. Government
Buildings, Dublin.

The first Government of the new State was headed by William T. Cosgrave of the *Cumann na nGaedheal* (later *Fine Gael*) party. Cosgrave set about establishing an administration which would enable the country to recover from the ravages of war. The Government's founding of the *Electricity Supply Board* in 1927 and the opening of the Shannon hydro-electric scheme marked an important stage in the country's economic development.

Éamon de Valera led the *Fianna Fáil* party which drew support from those who had opposed the treaty. *Fianna Fáil* came to power in 1932 with de Valera as head of Government. A dispute over continuous land payments to the British Government led to the 'economic war' of 1932–38. Trade with Britain was restricted and considerable hardship resulted. In 1937 de Valera introduced a new constitution declaring Ireland to be a sovereign, independent, democratic state.

Ireland remained neutral during the Second World War, 1939–45. Although the wartime years were a period of shortages and difficulties, the country was spared the worst effects of the conflict.

Fianna Fáil lost office in the 1948 election after sixteen continuous years in power. The new administration, headed by John A. Costello, was an inter-party Government formed by *Fine Gael*, *Labour* and other parties. In 1948 the **Republic of Ireland Act** was passed, severing the last constitutional links with Britain.

Costello's Government fell in 1951 after a controversy over the future direction of social policy. De Valera led another *Fianna Fáil* administration for the next three years and Costello returned to Government in 1954.

Ireland was admitted to the **United Nations** in 1955. Irish delegations have played an active role in UN affairs over the years and from 1958 onwards Irish troops have been involved in a large number of UN peacekeeping operations. *Fianna Fáil* regained power in the 1957 election and Éamon de Valera resigned the leadership of the party in 1959 to serve as President of Ireland. He was succeeded by Sean Lemass under whose premiership the country began a period of rapid economic expansion.

The signing of the Anglo-Irish free-trade agreement in 1965 led to significant developments in trading patterns and to industrial expansion. Even more importantly, Ireland became a member of the **European Community** in 1973.

In the years since 1969 the crisis in Northern Ireland has affected the Irish State. Successive Governments have sought to develop a solution to the problem which will provide lasting peace and stability. Profound change has affected the political, social, economic and cultural life of the country in the intervening quarter century.

■ *Name of State*
The Constitution provides (Article 4) that the name of the State is *Éire*, or in the English language, *Ireland*. Normal practice is to restrict the use of the name *Éire* to texts in the Irish language and to use *Ireland* in all English-language texts, with corresponding translations for texts in other languages. The Republic of Ireland Act of 1948 provides for the description of the State as the *Republic of Ireland* but this provision has not changed

Name, Symbols and National Day

the usage *Ireland* as the name of the State in the English language.

The etymology of the name *Éire* is uncertain and various theories have been advanced. There is no doubt but that it is a name of considerable antiquity. It first appears as *Ierne* in Greek geographical writings which may be based on sources as early as the 5th century BC. In Ptolemy's map (c AD 150) the name appears as *Iouernia*; some such form was transliterated into Latin as *Iuverna*. The standard Latin form, *Hibernia*, first appears in the works of Caesar, who seems to have confused it with the Latin word *hibernus* (wintry). *Ériu*, the Old Irish form of *Éire*, was current in the earliest Irish literature. The modern English word *Ireland* derives from the Irish word *Éire* with the addition of the Germanic word *land*.

In mythology, *Ériu* was one of three divine eponyms for Ireland, together with Banba and Fodla. The idea of Ireland as a heroine reappears as a common motif in later literature in both Irish and English.

■ *Flag*

The national flag is a tricolour of green, white and orange. The tricolour is rectangular in shape, the width being twice the depth. The three colours are of equal size, vertically disposed, and the green is displayed next to the staff. The flag was first introduced by Thomas Francis Meagher during the revolutionary year of 1848 as an emblem of the **Young Ireland** movement, and it was often seen displayed at meetings alongside the French tricolour.

The green represents the older Gaelic and Anglo-Norman element in the population,

37. *The national flag.*

while the orange represents the Protestant planter stock, supporters of William of Orange. The meaning of the white was well expressed by Meagher when he introduced the flag. "The white in the centre", he said, "signifies a lasting truce between the 'Orange' and the 'Green' and I trust that beneath its folds the hands of the Irish Protestant and the Irish Catholic may be clasped in heroic brotherhood."

It was not until the Rising of 1916, when it was raised above the General Post Office in Dublin, that the tricolour came to be regarded as the national flag. It rapidly gained precedence over any flag which had existed before, and its use as a national flag is enshrined in the Constitution.

■ *Emblem*

The harp has been regarded as the official symbol or coat of arms of Ireland since medieval times. As such it is depicted alongside the coats of arms of a dozen or more medieval European kingdoms on a single folio of the Wijnbergen roll of arms compiled about 1270. The harp is found on the banners of the Irish brigades, which were formed in the armies of continental European countries during the seventeenth and eighteenth centuries.

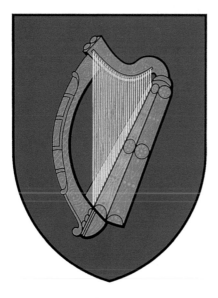

38. The arms of Ireland.

39. The national anthem.

The heraldic harp is invariably used by the Government, its agencies and its representatives at home and abroad. It is engraved on the seal matrix of the office of President as well as on the reverse of the coinage of the state. It is also emblazoned on the distinctive flag of the President — a gold harp with silver strings on an azure field.

The model for the artistic representation of the heraldic harp is the 14th century harp now preserved in the Museum of Trinity College Dublin, popularly known as the Brian Boru harp.

■ Anthem

The text of *The Soldier's Song (Amhrán na bhFíann)*, consisting of three stanzas and a chorus, was written in 1907 by Peadar Kearney, who also composed the music together with Patrick Heeney. It was first published in the newspaper, *Irish Freedom*, in 1912. The chorus, of which the words and music are given above, was formally adopted as the National Anthem in 1926, displacing the earlier Fenian anthem, *God Save Ireland*. A section of the National Anthem (consisting of the first four bars followed by the last

PAGE 35

five) is also the Presidential Salute.

■ *National Day*
The national day is St Patrick's Day, the 17th of March.

Constitution

The basic law of the State is the Constitution of Ireland (Bunreacht na hÉireann) adopted by referendum in 1937. It is the successor to the Constitution of *Dáil Éireann* (1919) and the Constitution of the Irish Free State (1922). The Constitution states that all legislative, executive and judicial powers of Government derive under God from the people. It sets out the form of government and defines the powers of the President, of the two Houses of the Oireachtas (Parliament), and of the Government. It defines the structure and powers of the Courts, and it contains a number of directive principles of social policy for the general guidance of the *Oireachtas*.

The Constitution regulates the method of election of the President and defines the President's powers in relation to the two Houses of the Oireachtas and the Government. It also defines the system of Courts and regulates the appointment of the judiciary.

The Constitution sets out the fundamental rights of the citizen. The definition of rights covers five broad headings: Personal Rights, The Family, Education, Private Property and Religion.

Personal Rights: the Constitution declares that all citizens are equal before the law, it guarantees to defend and vindicate the personal rights of citizens, it provides that there will be no deprivation of liberty except in accordance with law, it provides for the right of *Habeas Corpus*, it guarantees the inviolability of citizens' dwellings except in accordance with law, it guarantees the liberty to express freely one's convictions and opinions, the right to assemble peaceably and without arms, and the right to form associations and unions. The Supreme Court has identified additional personal rights which, although not listed in the Constitution, are protected by it, such as the right to travel and to marry and the right of access to the Courts.

The Family: through the Constitution the State guarantees to protect the family and the institution of marriage.

Education: the State recognises the primacy of the family in the education of children and undertakes to provide for free primary education and to supplement and aid private educational initiative with due regard to the rights of parents.

Private Property: the right to hold private property is guaranteed and is subject only to the exigencies of the common good.

Religion: the Constitution guarantees freedom of conscience and the free profession and practice of religion, subject only to public order and morality.

The Constitution may be amended only by an Act of the *Oireachtas*, the Bill for which has been approved by the people in a referendum after being passed by both **Houses of the Oireachtas**. Up to 1993 the people had approved 11 Bills in referenda to amend the Constitution.

Citizens, and in certain cases non-citizens, have the right to apply to the Courts to protect from infringement their rights under the Constitution. They may also apply to have a judgement pronounced as to whether legislation is compatible with the Constitution, provided the legislation affects, or is likely to affect, the person challenging it. Moreover, the President may, before signing a Bill, refer it to the Supreme Court for a decision on its compatibility with the Constitution. These procedures have been employed on a number of occasions.

President, Parliament and Government

Ireland is a parliamentary democracy. The national parliament (in the Irish language, *Oireachtas*) consists of the President (*an tUachtarán*) and two Houses: a House of Representatives (*Dáil Éireann*) and a Senate (*Seanad Éireann*). The functions and powers of the President, Dáil and Seanad derive from the Constitution of Ireland and law.

■ *The President*
Under the Constitution, the President of Ireland (*Uachtarán na hÉireann*) is elected by the direct vote of the people. Every citizen of thirty-five years of age or over is eligible for the office. Every citizen who has a right to vote at an election for members of Dáil Éireann has the right to vote at an election for President. The President's term of office is seven years. A President can be

re-elected once only. Presidents elected since the creation of the office in 1937 have been Dr. Douglas Hyde (1938–1945), Seán T. Ó Ceallaigh (1945–1959), Éamon de Valera (1959–1973), Erskine Childers (1973–1974), Cearbhall Ó Dálaigh (1974–1976), Dr. Patrick Hillery (1976–1990). President Mary Robinson was elected on 7 November, 1990.

The President is Head of State only and does not have executive functions. The Constitution, however, envisages the President as more than a ceremonial Head of State. It gives the President certain powers that make the President in effect the guardian of the Constitution.

The President normally acts on the advice and authority of the Government. On the nomination of Dáil Éireann the President appoints the *Taoiseach* (Prime Minister). On the advice of the *Taoiseach* and with the prior approval of *Dáil Éireann* the President appoints members of the Government. On the advice of the *Taoiseach*, the President accepts the resignation or terminates the appointment of a member of the Government. *Dáil Éireann* is summoned and

40. *Áras an Uachtaráin: the official residence of the President.*

dissolved by the President on the advice of the *Taoiseach*.

Before a Bill may become law, it must have the President's signature.

The President has certain discretionary powers. First, the President may, after consultation with the Council of State, an advisory body to the President, refer any Bill to the Supreme Court for a decision as to whether it contains anything repugnant to the Constitution.

Secondly, if a majority of the Seanad and not less than one-third of the *Dáil* petition the President to decline to sign a Bill on the grounds that it contains a proposal of such national importance that the will of the people thereon ought to be ascertained, the President may accede to the request after consultation with the Council of State. In these circumstances the President may sign the Bill only when the proposal has been approved by the people in a referendum or by a new Dáil after a dissolution and a General Election.

The President has one power which may be exercised at his or her absolute discretion. This allows the President to refuse to dissolve the *Dáil* on the advice of a *Taoiseach* who has ceased to retain the support of a majority in the *Dáil*.

The supreme command of the defence forces is vested in the President.

There is no Vice-President of Ireland. If the President dies in office, or is incapacitated, or is abroad, or is removed from office or fails to carry out functions enjoined on the office by the Constitution, the Constitution provides for a Commission to act in his or her place. The Commission would consist of the Chief Justice, the

Chairman of *Dáil Éireann*, and the Chairman of *Seanad Éireann*.

■ *Parliament*

The sole power of making laws for the State is vested in Parliament. Government policy and administration may be examined and criticised in both Houses; but under the Constitution the Government is responsible to the Dáil alone. In the passage of legislation the primacy of the Dáil is clearly shown in relation to Money Bills, on which the Seanad is empowered only to make recommendations (not amendments) and these must be made within twenty-one days.

■ *Dáil Éireann*

At present Dáil Éireann has 166 members called *Teachtaí Dála* (TDs). Members are returned by the forty-one constituencies into which the country is divided. Under present arrangements, twelve constituencies return three members each, fifteen constituencies return four members each, and fourteen constituencies return five members each. No constituency may return less than three members. Under the Constitution the number of members shall from time to time be fixed by law, but the total number of members of Dáil Éireann shall not be fixed at less than one member for each thirty thousand of the population, or at more than one member for each twenty thousand of the population. The ratio of elected members to population shall, as far as is practicable, be the same for each constituency throughout the country. The Houses of the Oireachtas must revise the constituencies at least once every twelve years.

41. The President,
Mrs. Mary Robinson,
following her
inauguration at
Dublin Castle.

■ *Seanad Éireann*

Seanad Éireann has sixty members. Eleven members are nominated directly by the Taoiseach. Forty-three members are elected from five panels of candidates — *The Cultural and Educational Panel, The Agricultural Panel, The Labour Panel, The Industrial and Commercial Panel* and *The Administrative Panel*. Each panel consists of persons with knowledge and practical experience of the interests represented by the panel. The remaining six members are elected by two universities — three by the National University of Ireland and three by the University of Dublin. The powers of the Seanad, as defined by the Constitution, are in general less than those of the Dáil. It has complementary powers with the Dáil in broad areas such as the removal from office of a President or a judge; the declaration and termination of a state of emergency; the initiation of Bills other than Money Bills; and the annulment of statutory instruments. The Seanad has prior or exclusive powers in other areas, however. A petition to the President to decline to sign a Bill until the matter can be put before the people in a referendum requires the assent of a majority of the members of the Seanad (and not less than one-third of the members of the Dáil). In cases where the Government requires that a Bill be signed earlier than the fifth day after it has been presented to the President, as is laid down in the Constitution, the Government needs the concurrence of the Seanad. A private Bill, where it is intended to promote the particular interest or benefit of any person or locality, as distinct from a measure of public policy,

41. The President, Mrs. Mary Robinson, following her inauguration at Dublin Castle.

must be introduced in the Seanad. After it has been passed by the Seanad the Bill is dealt with in the Dáil and, when and if agreed to, it is sent to the President for signing.

■ *Parliamentary Committees*

The Houses of the Oireachtas also operate through a system of parliamentary committees.

The Committees on *Procedure and Privileges* and of *Selection* of each House and the *Joint (Dáil and Seanad) Services Committee* deal with the efficient running of the Houses.

The Dáil Committee of *Public Accounts* and the *Joint Committee on Commercial State-sponsored Bodies* are concerned with the functions of Parliament relating to public spending and the monitoring of State-sponsored bodies.

The Dáil Select Committees on *Social Affairs, Finance and General Affairs, Enterprise and Economic Strategy, Legislation and Security* and the Joint Committee on *Foreign Affairs* deal with some of the functions of the Oireachtas in relation to legislation.

Committees dealing with specialised subjects include the Joint Committee on *Women's Rights* and *An Comhchoiste don Ghaeilge* (Joint Committee on the Irish language).

The *Committees of Selection* (of each House) nominate members to serve on their respective committees and have the power to discharge such members from time to time for non-attendance or at their own request, and they have the power to appoint other members to replace those discharged.

■ *Government*

The executive powers of the State are exercised by, or on the authority of, the Government. The Constitution provides that the Government shall consist of not less than seven and not more than fifteen members. The Taoiseach, Tánaiste and Minister for Finance must be members of the Dáil. The other members of the Government may be members of the Dáil or Seanad, but not more than two may be members of the Seanad. The Government acts collectively and is responsible to the Dáil.

The Taoiseach is appointed by the President on the nomination of the Dáil. He must resign if he ceases to retain the support of a majority in the Dáil.

The Taoiseach assigns Departments of State to members of the Government. Usually, each member of the Government heads one Department of State, but occasionally a Minister is responsible for more than one Department. Ministers of State, who are not members of the Government, assist Government Ministers in their Parliamentary and Departmental work. The maximum number of Ministers of State is fixed by law at seventeen.

The Taoiseach nominates one member of the Government to be Tánaiste. The Tánaiste acts in place of the Taoiseach if the Taoiseach is temporarily absent or becomes incapacitated.

The Attorney General, while not a member of the Government, acts as legal advisor to the Government and may attend Cabinet meetings. The Attorney General's tenure of office is normally coterminous with that of the Government.

■ *Voting in Elections and Referenda*

Opportunities to vote arise in five decision-making procedures:

— the election of the President every seven years;

— Dáil (parliamentary) elections, at least every five years;

— referenda on proposed Constitutional amendments;

— the election of representatives to the European Parliament, every five years;

— elections to local authorities, usually every five years.

Resident citizens over the age of 18 years may vote at Dáil, Presidential, local and European elections, and referenda. British citizens living in Ireland may vote at Dáil, European and local elections. European Union citizens may vote at European and local elections. All residents, regardless of citizenship, may vote at local elections.

The electoral system is proportional representation by means of a single transferable vote (PR-STV) in multi-member constituencies.

■ *Dáil Elections*

Voting in Dáil elections is by secret ballot; postal voting is confined to members of the defence forces and civil servants and their spouses serving abroad. The system of voting used can be described as follows: The voter marks the ballot paper by placing the figure "1" opposite the name of the candidate of his or her first choice and, if the voter wishes, "2" is placed opposite the name of the second choice, and so on.

The elector is, in effect, telling the returning officer "I wish to vote for A, but if that candidate does not need my vote or has no chance of being elected, transfer my vote to B; if B in turn does not need my vote, or in turn has no chance of election, transfer my vote to C". At the opening of the count, the ballot papers are mixed together and then sorted according to the first preferences recorded for the candidates. The total number of valid papers is counted, and the electoral quota is calculated. The quota is the smallest number of votes necessary to secure the election of a candidate. The quota is established according to the formula:

$$\frac{\text{Total valid votes}}{\text{number of seats} + 1} + 1$$

Thus, if there were 40,000 valid votes and four seats to be filled, the quota for election would be 8,001 and only four candidates could reach the quota.

If, on the first count, no candidate has reached the quota, the candidate who received the lowest number of votes is eliminated and his or her votes are transferred to the candidate for whom a second preference is recorded. If a candidate receives more than the quota required for election, his or her surplus votes are transferred to the remaining candidates in accordance with the subsequent preferences expressed by the electors.

When the number of remaining candidates who have neither been elected nor eliminated corresponds to the number of vacancies to be filled, those candidates are declared elected. This applies even though the remaining candidates may not have reached the quota.

■ Seanad Elections

An election for the *Seanad* takes place not later than ninety days after a dissolution of Dáil Éireann. The voting system used is proportional representation by secret postal ballot.

The electorate for the forty-three members of the Seanad elected from panels of candidates, numbers just over 1,100. The electorate comprises the members of the newly-elected Dáil, the members of the outgoing Seanad, and the members of every council of a county or county borough. There is a separate election for each of the five panels. The electorate for the six members elected from the universities consists of every citizen who has received a degree (other than an honorary one) from those universities and who has attained the age of eighteen years and is registered as an elector.

■ Political Parties

Fianna Fáil, Fine Gael, Labour, The Progressive Democrats, Democratic Left, and the *Green Party* are represented in the *Dáil*.

Fianna Fáil

Fianna Fáil, the Republican Party, was founded by Éamon de Valera in 1926. Its aims are to secure the unity and independence of Ireland as a republic, to restore the Irish language, to develop a distinctive national life in accordance with Irish traditions and ideals, and to make the resources and wealth of Ireland subservient to the needs and welfare of all the people of Ireland. Its policy also includes the provision of employment for the maximum number of people.

Fianna Fáil
The Republican Party

(Text courtesy Fianna Fáil)

Fianna Fáil was in government in 1932–1948, 1951–1954, 1957–1973, 1977–1981, in 1982 and from 1987 to December 1994. Its leaders have been Éamon de Valera, 1926–1959, Sean Lemass, 1959–1966, Jack Lynch, 1966–1979, Charles Haughey, 1979–1992, Albert Reynolds, 1992–1994, and Bertie Ahern, from November, 1994. Its achievements have included the consolidation of Irish independence, promulgation of the Constitution in 1937, maintenance of Irish neutrality in the Second World War, construction of a domestic industrial base, redistribution of agricultural land, the introduction and extension of housing and social assistance programmes, the opening up of Ireland to trade and investment, negotiating entry into the EEC and participation in the EU, including a massive increase in EU funding and the attraction of high technology industry and financial services to Ireland. In the 1992 to 1994 Government, in which *Fianna Fáil* was the main partner, the Joint Declaration on peace in Northern Ireland was signed by the Taoiseach and the British Prime Minister at Downing Street on 15 December, 1993.

Fianna Fáil is a broad based party with strong representation in both urban and rural Ireland. Since 1932 it has consistently been the largest party in the Dáil, and at the election in November, 1992 won 39% of the popular vote. It holds 67 out of the 166 seats in Dáil Éireann. Fianna Fáil is part of the European Democratic Alliance in the European Parliament. The Party's Head Office is at 13 Upper Mount Street, Dublin 2.

(Text courtesy Fine Gael)

Fine Gael

Fine Gael won over 25% of the total votes cast in the general election of November, 1992. The party holds 47 out of the 166 seats in *Dáil Éireann*, and is the largest party in the Government. The leader of *Fine Gael* is An Taoiseach, John Bruton.

Fine Gael was founded in 1933 by the coming together of a number of parties. The predominant party in this amalgamation was *Cumann na nGaedheal*. *Cumann na nGaedheal* had been founded in 1923 to sustain the Government of the infant Free State in its efforts to build and develop the new nation on the basis of the treaty negotiated a few months earlier. The *Cumann na nGaedheal* party governed from the foundation of the State until 1932. *Fine Gael* has committed itself to an ideal which was shared by *Cumann na nGaedheal* of developing a wider, pluralistic sense of Irish nationalism.

Fine Gael policy is based on the principles of the encouragement of enterprise combined with social justice and with decision-making devolved to the appropriate level, as well as on the ideal of reconciliation with the people of Northern Ireland. *Fine Gael* favours a planned approach to encourage expansion to counteract the effect of world recession. This is to be done by a mixture of State encouragement for private enterprise and effort and direct State involvement. It has as its immediate objectives improved access for young people and women to decision-making, greater tax equity, fairer opportunities in education and the maintenance or improvement of social welfare provisions.

Fine Gael is also committed to the development and unification of the European Union. Along with its fellow Christian Democrats in the European People's Party, *Fine Gael* seeks solutions on a European level to the problems and challenges of the 1990's. The EPP is the second largest group in the European Parliament and is a strong advocate of European integration. Fine Gael's Head Office is at 51 Upper Mount Street, Dublin 2.

Labour Party

(Text courtesy
The Labour Party)

The *Labour Party* is represented in Dáil Éireann, Seanad Éireann and in the European Parliament as a member of the Party of European Socialists (PES).

The Party was founded in 1912 at a conference of the Irish Trade Union Congress in Clonmel under the inspiration of James Connolly, Jim Larkin and William O'Brien.

It is the oldest political party in Ireland and through its affiliation to the Socialist International is a sister party of the Social Democratic and Labour Party in Northern Ireland.

The *Labour Party* seeks to build a society free from deprivation and based on the principles of democracy, equality, participation and co-operation.

The *Labour Party* has twelve affiliated trade unions representing 50% of all trade union members in the State.

Since its foundation, the *Labour Party* has taken part in seven coalition Governments, the present one of which dates from late 1994.

At the General Election of 1992 the Party won 19.3% of the votes and 33 seats which was its highest ever. This enabled the Party to enter Government early in 1993. In that Government the *Labour Party* contributed to the negotiation of the Joint Declaration on peace in Northern Ireland signed by the Taoiseach and British Prime Minister at Downing Street on 15 December, 1993.

In 1990 Labour T.D.s and Senators nominated Mary Robinson as President of Ireland. She went on to win the election and became Ireland's first woman President.

The leader of the *Labour Party* is Dick Spring who is also Tánaiste and Minister for Foreign Affairs. The Party Head Office is at 17 Ely Place, Dublin 2.

The Progressive Democrats

The Progressive Democrats were formed in 1985. There are eight members of the parliamentary party, six Dáil Deputies and two Senators.

The leader of the Progressive Democrats is Mary Harney, the first woman leader of a political party in the history of the State. Mary Harney was elected leader in October, 1993. She succeeded the founder of the Party, Desmond O'Malley.

The *Progressive Democrats* were established with the aim of providing Ireland with a modern, forward looking liberal party in the European mould. The party favours positive Government action to create an enterprise society and a review of the role of the State in the economic and social life of the country. The party supports the movement towards greater political and economic integration amongst the Member States of the European Union.

The party was a member of the Coalition Government of 1989 to 1991 and is the second largest opposition party in Dáil

Éireann. Its headquarters are at 25 South Frederick Street, Dublin 2.

Democratic Left

Democratic Left was founded in 1992.

The party has five members in the Dáil and one member in the Seanad. In the November, 1992 General Election it recorded 3% of the first-preference vote. The party is organised in the Republic of Ireland and Northern Ireland and is represented on a total of 19 local authorities. Democratic Left entered government as part of the coalition formed in December, 1994.

Among the principal objectives of *Democratic Left* are:
— the development of a pluralist, socialist society in Ireland;
— commitment to a positive neutrality for Ireland and global collective security;
— the incorporation of ecological principles into social, economic and political decision-making.

Party policy is decided at the Annual Delegate Conference which also elects the party leader and a National Executive Committee of 20 members.

Democratic Left is particularly committed to the achievement of gender equality in society and in its own internal structures. There is a minimum 40% gender quota on the party's NEC. *Democratic Left* believes that neither traditional unionism nor traditional nationalism can provide a solution to the problems in Northern Ireland. The party belongs to a "third strand" of political opinion which emphasises equal recognition of and respect for the opposing national allegiances which have been at the heart of the conflict in Northern Ireland, and supports

Progressive Democrats
AN PÁIRTÍ DAONLATHACH

(Text courtesy The Progressive Democrats)

(Text courtesy Democratic Left)

the concept of weighted-majority decision making at central and local level.

The party is committed to the development of the European Union along democratic lines but is opposed to the emergence of an EU military super-power.

The leader of *Democratic Left* is Proinsias De Rossa, Minister for Social Welfare. The Party's address is c/o Dáil Éireann, Kildare Street, Dublin 2.

(Text courtesy
The Green Party)

The Green Party
The *Green Party*/Comhaontas Glas was founded in 1982 from an alliance of social movements and protest groups. The Party's electoral breakthrough came in 1989 when the first Green TD was elected. This was followed by further electoral successes in local government elections, with another major breakthrough coming in the 1994 European elections when the electorate sent two Green MEPs to Brussels.

The motto of the Green Party is, *Think Globally, Act Locally*, and it puts this into practice by its activities on a number of social and environmental issues in Ireland. It is linked with the European-wide Green movement, and with them is working for a sustainable, just and ecological world.

The Party has no leaders, with all positions within it rotating after one year. Experience has shown that an open, non-hierarchial party works the best. The Party's headquarters are at 5A Upper Fownes St., Dublin 2.

Finance

Under the Constitution, public monies can be expended to the extent and in the manner authorised by Dáil Éireann. The right of initiative in relation to public finances is

confined solely to the Government: the Dáil may not pass any measure for the appropriation of public monies unless the purpose of the expenditure has been recommended to the Dáil by the Government.

Central Government expenditure falls into two broad categories — non-voted expenditure which the Dáil has declared by law is to be paid without annual reference to the Dáil, and which consists primarily of funds to service the national debt; and voted expenditure, which accounts for the majority of Government expenditure and finances the running of Government Departments. The money for this second category is voted by the Dáil through the Dáil Committee of

42. Portrait by Sir John Lavery, commissioned for the first issue of the State's currency notes, 1928.

Public Accounts. The Accounting Officer, normally the Secretary of each Government Department, is personally responsible for the safeguarding of public funds and property under his control.

■ *Taxation*
Subject to certain exceptions and exemptions, a person resident in the State is liable to income tax on total income. After allowances and deductions are provided for, tax is applied to remaining income at a standard rate of 27% and a single higher rate of 48%. The principal components of tax revenue are: indirect taxes, 38%; income tax, 32%; social security contributions, 15%; corporate taxation, 8%; and capital and property taxes, 4%.

The Civil Service

The legal basis for the present system of central public administration is contained in the *Ministers and Secretaries Act* of 1924 and its eleven subsequent amendments. The Act provides for a statutory classification of the functions of Government under the various Departments and Offices of State. There are sixteen Government Departments for which fifteen Ministers of Government, assisted by seventeen Ministers of State, have responsibility in all matters. The day-to-day management and administration of a Department's functions is entrusted to the Secretary of the Department who is a permanent civil servant, appointed by the Government.

The civil service is independent in the performance of its duties and has no involvement in party politics. Party political activity is strictly forbidden for all middle and high-ranking civil servants.

Recruitment to the civil service is by open public competition administered by the independent Civil Service Commission. Staff are recruited at a number of different grades up to middle management level.

The civil service comprises a number of grade categories with different functions. These functions cover, broadly, four categories of duties: the *administrative* grades have responsibility for policy formulation; the *professional* grades provide specialist knowledge and skills within the civil service; the *executive* grades are involved in the implementation of policy decisions; the *clerical* grades are responsible for general duties. There are some 30,000 people employed in the civil service.

Teachers and members of An Garda Síochána (police force) and staff of local authorities and of the health services belong to the wider public service, rather than the civil service. Their salaries are also, however, paid from central Government funds, through the Departments of Education, Justice, Environment, Health, and Defence respectively.

■ *Departments of State*
The *Department of An Taoiseach* provides the secretariat to the Government and assists the Taoiseach in the carrying out of his constitutional and legal functions. The Department has responsibility for the National Economic and Social Council, the Government Information Services and the Central Statistics Office. It has responsibility in regard to the administration of all public services which do not fall within the remit of another Government Department while also being charged with the custody of public

43. *The centre of Dublin.*

44. Wexford; a modern town of Viking origin. The adjoining farmland is typical of the region.

archives and state papers.

The *Department of Finance* has responsibility for the administration and guardianship of the public finances of the State. It is concerned with the raising and the provision of money for State purposes, the control of public expenditure, and social and economic planning. It is responsible for the coordination and the improvement of personnel and management functions in the public service. It is also responsible for other central Government services such as the Office of the Revenue Commissioners and the Office of Public Works.

The *Department of Agriculture, Food and Forestry* is concerned with all aspects of the agricultural, food and forestry industries. It operates a nationwide network of inspectors, research facilities and disease eradication schemes. The Department is concerned with the foundation and the operation of land policy and it also deals with the administration and implementation of European Union agricultural policies.

The *Department of Arts, Culture and the Gaeltacht* has responsibility for the formulation of policy relating to arts, culture and the national heritage as well as the promotion of the Irish language and of Irish-speaking regions.

The *Department of Defence* is responsible for the external security of the State. This involves the administration, recruitment, regulation and organisation of the army including the air corps, the naval service, as well as civil defence.

The *Department of Education* administers, oversees and finances primary, secondary and third-level education services and operates the State examination system for schools. The Department also has responsibility for the formulation of policy with regard to sport and recreation.

The *Department of Enterprise and Employment* is responsible for policy formulation in the areas of industrial development, science and technology, commerce, employment and consumer protection. It also has responsibility for manpower policy which involves the provision of vocational training and work experience programmes.

The *Department of the Environment* is responsible for the coordination of local government administration in the areas of housing, water, sanitation, fire services and planning.

The *Department of Equality and Law Reform* is charged with promoting equality of opportunity within the State and has responsibility for instituting law reform measures, particularly in the areas of equality and family law.

The *Department of Foreign Affairs'* primary function is to advise the Government on Ireland's foreign relations and to act as the channel of official communication with foreign Governments and official organisations. The Department is responsible for diplomatic representation abroad and for the implementation of Ireland's aid programme for developing countries.

The *Department of Health* has responsibility for the services provided by the regional health authorities. It also deals with areas outside the remit of the health authorities, e.g. voluntary hospitals. It reviews existing services and initiates proposals for new services.

The *Department of Justice* has

responsibility for the internal security of the State. It has responsibility for the courts, the prison service and An Garda Síochána (police force).

The *Department of the Marine* is responsible for policy issues in relation to the fishing and marine related industries, shipping, marine research and technology, aquaculture, marine safety and general marine conservation policy.

The *Department of Social Welfare* is charged with the administration of the social insurance and the social assistance schemes within the State social security system.

The *Department of Tourism and Trade* has responsibility for the formulation of policies in relation to tourism and trade matters.

The *Department of Transport, Energy and Communications* is charged with policy formulation in the areas of aviation, rail and road transport, energy, petroleum and minerals exploration, as well as postal, radio and telecommunications policies.

Many Departments also have responsibility for State-sponsored companies entrusted with the implementation of policy. There are also a number of other organisations within the civil service:

The *Office of the Revenue Commissioners* is responsible for the administration, enforcement and collection of taxes and duties.

The *Office of Public Works* provides accommodation for Government Departments and offices, police stations, post offices and primary schools; it undertakes civil engineering projects on behalf of the State as well as managing national monuments and public parks.

Other State services include the Government Supplies Agency, the Central Statistics Office, the Valuation and Ordnance Survey Office, the State Laboratory, the Office of the Comptroller and Auditor General, the Office of the Attorney General and the Government Information Services.

There are approximately 100 State-sponsored bodies employing about 75,000 people. They are engaged in a wide range of activities, but the major organisations operate in the following areas:

State-Sponsored Bodies

■ *Public Utilities*
The *Electricity Supply Board* is responsible for all electricity generation and supply. *An Post* and *Telecom Éireann* provide mail and telecommunications services respectively. *Bord Gáis* (Irish Gas Board) is responsible for the supply of natural gas. *RTÉ*, the radio and television network, runs the national television and radio service.

■ *Transport*
The public road and rail transport system is operated by the *CIE* group of companies. *Iarnród Éireann* (Irish Rail) operates the nationwide railway system for passengers and freight, including the *Dublin Area Rapid Transit (DART)* network. *Bus Átha Cliath* (Dublin Bus) operates urban bus services in the Greater Dublin area. *Bus Éireann* (Irish Bus) operates a network of bus services outside Dublin city. *Aer Rianta* manages international airports at Dublin, Cork and Shannon. *Aer Lingus*, the Irish international airline, provides international air services.

■ *Other Trading Companies*
IFI manufactures agricultural fertilizers. *The Irish National Petroleum Corporation* deals in the international oil market and operates its own refinery. *Bord na Móna*, the *Irish Peat Development Board*, is responsible for the development and processing of Ireland's peat resources. *Coillte Teo.* is responsible for the commercial functions of the forest service.

■ *Promotional Agencies*
Forbairt is the agency responsible for developing indigenous industry. The *Industrial Development Agency — Ireland* is the agency responsible for attracting foreign investment into Ireland. *Bord Tráchtála* (The Irish Export Board) promotes Irish products in export markets and *Bord Fáilte* (Irish Tourist Board) markets Ireland as an international tourist destination.

Other State-sponsored bodies are engaged in the areas of education and research, public administration, fisheries and corporate finance. Within general policy guidelines laid down by the Government, State-sponsored bodies have significant autonomy. Although the Government or an individual Minister usually appoints members to the Boards or Councils of the bodies, they are not subject to detailed Ministerial control over day-to-day matters.

Local Government

The structure and functions of local government are under review. Changes are being made to strengthen and modernise the powers of authorities to provide greater flexibility and to ensure that local government structures are more relevant to local communities. It is intended, at the same time, to ensure that local government is more effective and efficient.

At present, the elected local authorities are the 29 County Councils, 5 County Borough Corporations, 5 Borough Corporations, 49 Urban District Councils and 26 boards of town commissioners.

■ *Membership and Election of Local Authorities*
The members of the various local authorities are elected according to a system of proportional representation for a period of five years. Any person who has reached the age of 18 is eligible to become a member and to vote at elections. County Councils vary in size from twenty to forty-eight members. County Borough Councils range from fifteen to fifty-two members. Borough Councils usually have twelve members; and Urban District Councils and Boards of Town Commissioners usually have nine.

■ *Management*
Each of the principal local authorities has a full time chief executive, the City or County Manager, with supporting administrative staff. The County Manager is responsible for the County Council and for every borough corporation, urban district council, board of town commissioners and every joint body whose functional area is within the county. The Manager's role and functions are set out in legislation which describes the relationship in terms of reserved functions (the elected council) and executive functions (the Manager).

Reserved functions are discharged by the elected members at their meetings; they comprise mainly decisions on important

45. Westlink Motorway, Ballymount, Co. Dublin

matters of policy and principle, including control over the financial affairs of the authority, the making of a development plan, and the making of bye-laws. Any function which is not a 'reserved' function is automatically an executive one to be performed by the Manager, but the elected members have various powers enabling them to oversee the activities of the Manager, and to give directions in certain circumstances. In turn, the Manager has a duty to advise and assist the elected members in the exercise of their functions.

■ *Services*

The services provided by the major local authorities can be described under the seven general headings of housing and building, road transportation and safety, water supply and sewerage, development incentives and controls, environmental protection, recreation and amenity, and miscellaneous services.

■ *Financing*

Expenditure by local authorities on the various services provided by them accounts for a sum corresponding to approximately 5.5% of GNP. This consists of current spending (approximately 65% of the total) and capital expenditure (approximately 35%). Almost all of the capital spending is funded by State grants, covering the cost of major construction works on roads, water and sanitary services facilities, and much of the housing construction programme. Revenue (current) expenditure is financed through a combination of State grants, local rates on commercial and industrial property, and through fees, charges, rents and services provided by the local authorities.

■ *Regional Authorities*

Regional authorities — eight of which were established in 1994 — are statutory bodies comprising local elected representatives selected by constituent local authorities. Their main tasks are to promote the co-ordination of public services in their region and to review and advise on the implementation of EU Structural and Cohesion Funds Programmes.

■ *Health Boards*

For health purposes the country is divided into eight regions, each of which is administered by a Health Board. The Boards

46. Living area, St Patrick's County Home, Waterford.

47. Regional Technical College at Tallaght, Co. Dublin.

administer community care services, general hospital services and special hospital services.

■ *Regional Tourism Organisations*
There are seven regional tourism organisations, one of which is operated by Shannon Development (SFADCO — the development agency for the Shannon region). Each organisation is a public company, limited by guarantee. Membership is open to all persons within the region and to local authorities, clubs, associations, and other relevant groups.

■ *Vocational Education Committees*
Vocational Education Committees provide technical and vocational education, including adult and continuing education. The committees have their own corporate status and are financed by State grants and by the local authorities.

■ *County Enterprise Boards*
A nationwide system of County Enterprise Boards has been established to provide a focus for enterprise and employment promotion at local level. The thirty-five Boards cover all urban and rural areas and are responsible for the development of enterprise plans, with particular reference to the promotion of small enterprises.

■ *Fisheries Boards*
The Central Fisheries Board and seven Regional Fisheries Boards are responsible for the protection, conservation, management and development of inland fisheries and of sea angling resources within their respective regions.

■ *Harbour Authorities*
Harbour authorities are responsible for the operation and maintenance of 25 commercial harbours under the general supervision of the Minister for the Marine.

The Ombudsman

The Ombudsman is empowered to investigate the actions of Government Departments, local authorities, health authorities, the postal and telecommunications service, and their officers. While the Office may initiate an investigation, it generally acts in response to complaints made by members of the public.

The Ombudsman is appointed by the President on the advice of the Government and is independent in the performance of his or her duties. The Office has its own investigative staff and is free to determine its own procedures. The Ombudsman reports annually to Dáil Éireann, but is free to make special reports at any time, in addition to annual reports. The term of office for the Ombudsman is six years.

Legal System

Irish law is based on Common Law as modified by subsequent legislation and by the Constitution of 1937. Statutes passed by the British parliament before 1921 have the force of law unless repealed by the Irish Parliament. In accordance with the Constitution, justice is administered in public in courts established by law. Judges are appointed by the President on the advice of the Government. They are invariably senior practising members of the legal profession. They are guaranteed independence in the exercise of their functions and can be removed from office for misbehaviour or incapacity only by resolution of both Houses

48. The Four Courts, Dublin.

of the Oireachtas (the National Parliament).

The court of summary jurisdiction is the **District Court**. The country is divided into 23 District Court districts. There are 46 judges of the District Court including the President of the District Court. A District Court is presided over by a District Court judge sitting without a jury. It tries minor criminal offences and has powers to impose fines of up to IR£1,000 or prison sentences up to a maximum of two years or both. The District Court also handles minor civil cases.

More serious cases are tried by the **Circuit Court**. The country is divided into eight Circuit Court circuits. There are 18 Judges of the Circuit Court including the President of the Court. The Circuit Court can try all criminal cases except murder, treason, piracy and allied offences. The jurisdiction of the Circuit Court in civil cases is limited to IR£30,000 unless both parties consent to its jurisdiction being unlimited. It also acts as an appeal court from the District Court. In criminal cases the Circuit Court is presided over by a judge sitting with a jury of twelve ordinary citizens. In other cases the Court is presided over by a judge sitting alone.

The **High Court** has full original jurisdiction and determining power in all matters of law or fact, civil or criminal. It can decide the validity of any law, having regard to the provisions of the Constitution. When trying criminal cases the High Court is known as the **Central Criminal Court**.

The High Court hears appeals from the Circuit Court in civil cases. In criminal cases, and in a limited number of civil cases, the Court is presided over by a judge sitting with a jury of twelve ordinary citizens. In other cases the Court is presided over by a judge sitting alone. There are 17 judges of the High Court including the President of the Court.

Legislation provides for the establishment of **Special Criminal Courts** whenever the Government is satisfied that the ordinary courts are inadequate to secure the effective administration of justice and the preservation of public peace and order. The Special Criminal Court is presided over by three serving judges drawn from the High Court, the Circuit Court and the District Court sitting together. There is no jury in the Special Criminal Court but, in most other respects, procedure governing this Court is the same as in criminal trials generally.

Criminal appeals from the Circuit Court, the Central Criminal Court and the Special Criminal Court are heard by the **Court of Criminal Appeal**, a court consisting of three judges drawn from the High Court and Supreme Court.

The **Supreme Court** is the court of final appeal. It consists of the Chief Justice, four other judges and, in an ex-officio capacity, the President of the High Court. The Court hears appeals from the High Court and the Court of Criminal Appeal. The Court is empowered to decide if the provisions of any statute are repugnant to the Constitution in the event of the President referring such provisions to the Court prior to the statute becoming law.

Although there is a limited right of private prosecution, most criminal prosecutions are instituted by the **Director of Public Prosecutions** on behalf of the State. The Director is a State official but is independent of Government in the performance of his or her functions.

The legal profession is divided into solicitors and barristers. Solicitors deal with legal business outside the courts such as transfer of land ownership, administration of the assets of deceased persons, and formation of limited companies. They also attend Court and while they have a right of audience before all courts, most of their work in this area comprises District Court cases and appeals to the Circuit Court. The **Incorporated Law Society of Ireland**, founded in 1852, acts as a regulatory body

for the solicitors' profession.

In the higher courts, cases are normally conducted by barristers who are either junior or senior counsel. Barristers are advised by, and in most cases can only be retained by, solicitors. The Benchers of the **Honorable Society of King's Inns** constitute the governing body of the Bar of Ireland.

Free legal aid is available, where necessary, in criminal cases and, on a more limited scale, in civil cases.

Police

The police force, **An Garda Síochána** (in English — Guardians of the Peace), was established in 1922 and is a national force of approximately 10,500 members. The general direction and control of the force is, subject to regulations made by the Minister for Justice, vested in a Commissioner appointed by the Government. The police force is an unarmed body, apart from some specialised units. The Headquarters of the force is in the Phoenix Park in Dublin. Under the Commissioner there is a Headquarters staff of two Deputy Commissioners, six Assistant Commissioners and the Surgeon to the force. One of the Assistant Commissioners is in charge of the Dublin Metropolitan Area, one is based in the Garda College and has responsibility for police training, and the others are based at Headquarters in charge of administrative departments. The ranks of An Garda Síochána are, in descending order, Assistant Commissioner, Chief Superintendent, Superintendent, Inspector, Sergeant and Garda. Entry to the force is at the rank of Garda. The force operates in 23 Divisions, each of which is divided into Districts and Sub-Districts. Divisions include regular and special forces for crime detection

49. *An Garda
    Síochána.*

and prevention. Divisions also carry out local police administrative functions. The police training centre is located at Templemore in Co. Tipperary. Garda trainees undergo a comprehensive two year training programme before entering the force. Among developed countries, Ireland has one of the lowest levels of serious crimes of violence while the crime detection rate is comparable to that of other countries.

The challenges facing the Garda Síochána in recent years have included the effects of social problems posed by rapid urbanisation. At the same time the policing of a circuitous border with Northern Ireland in co-operation with the defence forces has absorbed a considerable amount of the force's resources.

In 1989, the Garda Síochána participated in its first United Nations peace-keeping mission, with the dispatch of a 50 member contingent to Namibia. Since then the Gardaí have been involved in other such missions, most notably in Angola, Cambodia, Mozambique and South Africa. Garda contingents are currently serving with the UN in Cyprus and the former Yugoslavia.

The role of the Defence Forces consists of the following:–

1. to defend the State against armed aggression;
2. to aid the civil power when called upon (meaning in practice to assist *An Garda Síochána*, the police — a mainly unarmed force).
3. to participate in United Nations missions in the cause of international peace;
4. to provide a fishery protection service in accordance with the State's obligations as a member of the European Union.

Defence

The Forces may also be called upon to fulfil other duties e.g. search and rescue, air ambulance service, air transport, assistance on the occasion of natural or other disasters, assistance in connection with the maintenance of essential services, combatting oil pollution at sea.

■ *Recruitment*
All recruitment is on a voluntary basis. Recruits are enlisted to serve for five years in the Permanent Defence Force followed by seven years in the Front Line Reserve Defence Force.

■ *Structure*
The Forces consist of the Permanent Defence Force and the Reserve Defence Force. The **Permanent Defence Force**, which includes the regular Army, the Air Corps, and the Naval Service, has an approximate current strength of 13,000 personnel. The **Reserve Defence Force**, comprising the First Line Reserve (former members of the Permanent

Force), the F.C.A. (An Fórsa Cosanta Áitiúil — territorial second-line army reserve) and An Slua Muirí (the second-line naval reserve) has a total strength of about 16,200 personnel.

Under the Constitution, the supreme command of the Defence Forces is vested in the President, from whom all officers hold their commissions. Military command is exercised by the Government through the Minister for Defence. The Minister is aided and advised on matters relating to the Department by a **Council of Defence** consisting of two civilian and three military members, including the Chief of Staff.

The country is divided into four territorial commands, Eastern, Southern, Western and Curragh Commands. Defence Forces Headquarters are located in Dublin.

The **Army** has four infantry brigades, comprising nine battalions in total, and an infantry force of two battalions. Each brigade has a field artillery regiment and a squadron/company size unit for each of the support corps (Cavalry, Engineer, Signals,

50. The army on service with UNIFIL, Lebanon.

Supply and Transport, Military Police and Medical Corps). There are in addition special military establishments which include a Military College based in the Curragh, Co. Kildare, an Equitation School, situated in McKee Barracks, Dublin, an Army School of Music located in Cathal Brugha Barracks, Dublin and an Apprentice School at Devoy Barracks, Naas, Co. Kildare. The current strength of the Army is 10,900 personnel all ranks. The part-time reserve (*An Fórsa Cosanta Áitiúil*) has a strength in excess of 15,000 personnel and is organised into 18 infantry battalions, six field artillery regiments and a number of squadron/company size units of support corps.

The **Air Corps'** bases are at Casement Aerodrome, Baldonnel, Co. Dublin and at Gormanston Air Station, Co. Meath. Most of the Corps' technical and administrative services are located at Casement Aerodrome which is also the main centre for flying and technical training. Fixed-wing aircraft types in service include Fouga Magister armed jet trainers, SIAI Marchetti SF 260W armed piston-engined trainers, Cessna F 172 reconnaissance aircraft, CASA CN 235 maritime patrol aircraft and Beech Super Kingair and Gulfstream G IV aircraft for VIP transport. Alouette III, Dauphin and Gazelle helicopters are also used. The Air Corps has a current strength of about 1,000 personnel.

The **Naval Service** has six offshore patrol vessels and a helicopter patrol vessel which can carry one of the Dauphin helicopters

51. Naval Service L.E. Orla.

operated by the Air Corps. All vessels are based at Haulbowline, Co. Cork and are mainly engaged in fishery protection duties. At present there are approximately 1,100 personnel in the Naval Service. The part-time naval reserve, *An Slua Muirí*, has 400 personnel and is organised in five companies located at Cork, Waterford, Limerick and Dublin (two companies).

■ *Service with the United Nations*
Irish troops have participated in several United Nations peacekeeping missions since 1958. In July 1960, the first full unit of the Defence Forces to serve abroad, an infantry battalion, went to the Congo (now Zaire). Personnel are currently serving with peacekeeping missions in the Middle East (UNTSO), Lebanon (UNIFIL), Afghanistan/Pakistan (OSGAP), Cyprus (UNFICYP), Kuwait (UNIKOM), Western Sahara (MINURSO), the former Yugoslavia (UNPROFOR) and with the UN peacekeeping mission in Haiti (UNMIH).

■ *Financing*
Expenditure on the Defence Forces accounts for approximately 1.3% of GNP annually.

■ *Civil Defence*
Civil Defence provides community service and assistance throughout the country in support of primary emergency services. Ministerial responsibility for Civil Defence is assigned to the Minister of State at the Department of Defence. The Department's functions include planning and overall direction and control of civil defence activities at local authority level.
The organisation, recruitment and training

of Civil Defence units is the responsibility of the local authorities. Local units are formed mainly of volunteers who are trained and equipped to provide search, rescue and recovery in all weathers, crowd stewarding, first aid, fire-fighting, care of the homeless and radiation monitoring, amongst other tasks. The active strength of Civil Defence is approximately 6,000 persons.

Political Background

Parliamentary
Representation

Government

The Economy

Population

Services

53. *Taoiseach (Prime Minister of Ireland) John Bruton and British Prime Minister John Major present 'A New Framework for Agreement', Belfast.*

The Taoiseach is accompanied by Tánaiste (Deputy Prime Minister) and Minister for Foreign Affairs Dick Spring, and by Ministers Nora Owen and Proinsias De Rossa. Prime Minister Major is accompanied by the Secretary of State for Northern Ireland, Sir Patrick Mayhew.

Preceding page:
52. John Speed's Ireland (1612) — one of the first maps to include the province of Ulster in detail.

54. Participants in the inaugural meeting of the Forum for Peace and Reconciliation, Dublin.

Having opted to remain outside the provisions of the Anglo-Irish Treaty of 1921, Northern Ireland has since then been separately administered as part of the United Kingdom of Great Britain and Northern Ireland. The following is intended as a brief outline of the history and administration of Northern Ireland; it illustrates also the part played by the Irish Government in seeking an agreed resolution of the conflict. More detailed information may be found in the sources listed in the bibliography at the end of the book.

Political Background

The existing political division in Ireland dates from 1920–21. At that time, after centuries of British rule including 120 years when the country was governed as part of the United Kingdom, 26 of the 32 counties of Ireland gained independence. The remaining six counties were allowed to opt out and this area continued in political union with Britain as *Northern Ireland*. However, while the United Kingdom Parliament at Westminster continued to exercise sovereignty, power on a variety of matters was devolved to a local Parliament and Government established at Stormont in Belfast in 1920. From 1921 to 1972, although Northern Ireland elected members to the Westminster Parliament, the devolved Government at Stormont operated with virtual autonomy from London on local matters. Power remained exclusively in the hands of the Unionist party which drew its support from the majority community in the area which favoured union with Britain. The nationalist community — approximately one third of the population — shared the desire of the people of the rest of the island for

Irish unity. They had in practice no role in Government and they suffered systematic discrimination at local level in many areas, including voting rights, housing and employment. In 1969 non-violent campaigners for civil rights met with a hostile and repressive response from the Stormont authorities ushering in a period of sustained political crisis. In the early 1970's there was a revival of paramilitary activity by the IRA, which had occurred sporadically in earlier decades; there was also a corresponding growth in paramilitary violence by loyalist extremist groups. In a deteriorating security situation the local Northern Ireland Parliament and Government were prorogued in 1972 and the British Government assumed direct responsibility for all aspects of the government of Northern Ireland. Since then, with the exception of one brief period in 1974 when a local executive was established on a power-sharing basis, Northern Ireland has been governed under a system of direct rule under the authority of the Secretary of State for Northern Ireland who is a member of the British Cabinet.

■ *Anglo-Irish Intergovernmental Council, 1981*

In 1980, at a meeting in Dublin Castle between the then Taoiseach (Prime Minister of Ireland), Mr Charles J Haughey, and the former British Prime Minister, Mrs Margaret Thatcher, the British and Irish Governments reached agreement on a broadening of the scope of relations between the two parts of Ireland and between Britain and Ireland. This marked a significant new departure in Anglo-Irish relations and was followed in 1981 by the establishment of an Anglo-Irish

Intergovernmental Council. The Council provided a formal framework within which relations between the two countries could be conducted, with particular emphasis on facilitating progress towards a resolution of the Northern Ireland conflict.

New Ireland Forum, 1983/84

In 1983 the New Ireland Forum was established. This brought together over a year-long period the constitutional nationalist parties on the island — i.e. those opposed to violence as a means of achieving political objectives — for consultations on the manner in which lasting peace and stability could be established. In the course of its work, the Forum considered how unionist and nationalist identities and interests could be accommodated in a new Ireland. It also strongly rejected and condemned paramilitary organisations and "all who resort to terror and murder to achieve their ends".

Anglo-Irish Agreement, 1985

In November 1985 the then Taoiseach, Dr. Garret FitzGerald, and Mrs Thatcher signed the Anglo-Irish Agreement. The Agreement was subsequently deposited as an International Agreement with the United Nations. The Agreement has the aims of "promoting peace and stability in Northern Ireland; helping to reconcile the two major traditions in Ireland; creating a new climate of cooperation between the people of the two countries; and improving cooperation in combatting terrorism". An Intergovernmental Conference was established which enables the Irish Government to put forward views and proposals on stated aspects of Northern Ireland affairs and requires both Governments to make determined efforts to resolve any differences that may arise between them. The Conference is chaired jointly by a representative of each Government. The present Joint Chairmen are

55. British and Irish leaders announce the Joint Declaration on peace in Northern Ireland, London.

56. Views of Northern Ireland (clockwise from top left): Royal Avenue, Belfast; The Mountains of Mourne, Co. Down; Dunluce Castle, Co. Antrim; and Lough Melvin, Co. Fermanagh.

Facing page:
57. Derry, Northern Ireland's second city, by night.

Mr Dick Spring, Tánaiste (Deputy Prime Minister) and Minister for Foreign Affairs of Ireland, and Sir Patrick Mayhew, Secretary of State for Northern Ireland. The Conference meets on a regular basis and is serviced by a Joint Secretariat, located in Belfast, comprising civil servants from both Governments.

International Fund for Ireland

Under the terms of Article 10 of the Anglo-Irish Agreement, the Irish and British Governments established the International Fund for Ireland in 1986 "to promote economic and social advance and to encourage contact, dialogue and reconciliation between nationalists and unionists throughout Ireland". The contributors to the Fund are the United States, the European Union, Canada, Australia and New Zealand. In pursuit of its objectives, the Fund supports economic initiatives by private enterprise and community groups under various programme headings, with particular emphasis on improving the position of the most disadvantaged areas in Northern Ireland.

Round-Table Talks, 1991/92

In an effort to revive the political process, talks were convened by the two Governments in the course of 1991 and 1992. The talks were conducted on a three-stranded basis reflecting the three sets of relationships which underlie the Northern Ireland situation; viz. relationships within Northern Ireland, between the north and south of the island, and between the two islands. The four main constitutional political parties within Northern Ireland (the Social Democratic and Labour Party, the Ulster Unionist Party, the Democratic Unionist Party and the Alliance Party) participated in the talks. While the talks succeeded in identifying some common ground, it did not prove possible to reach over-all agreement.

Joint Declaration, 1993

The Joint Declaration on Northern Ireland, signed by the then Taoiseach, Mr Albert Reynolds, and the British Prime Minister, Mr John Major, on 15 December 1993, sets out the basic principles to be followed in establishing a framework for the settlement of political relationships in Ireland and between Ireland and Britain. Central to the Declaration is the statement that all questions relating to the pursuit of political objectives must be settled by peaceful and democratic means exclusively. The Declaration recognised, on behalf of the British Government, "that it is for the people of Ireland alone, by agreement between the two parts respectively, to exercise their right of self-determination on the basis of consent, freely and concurrently given, North and South, to bring about a united Ireland, if that is their wish". It recognised equally, on behalf of the Irish Government, that this right "must be achieved and exercised with and subject to the agreement and consent of a majority of the people in Northern Ireland". In the Declaration, the British Government stated that it had no selfish strategic or economic interest in Northern Ireland and that it would uphold the democratic wish of a greater number of the people there on the issue of whether they preferred to support the Union or a sovereign united Ireland. The primary interest of the

British Government is to see "peace, stability and reconciliation established by agreement among all the people who inhabit the island". The Irish Government confirmed that, in the event of an overall settlement and as part of a balanced constitutional accommodation, it would put forward and support proposals for changes in the Irish Constitution which would fully reflect the principle of consent in Northern Ireland.

■ *Paramilitary Ceasefires, 1994*
On 31 August, 1994 the IRA announced a complete cessation of all military activities. On 13 October the loyalist paramilitaries made a similar declaration.

■ *Forum for Peace and Reconciliation, 1994-*
The Forum for Peace and Reconciliation was established by the Irish Government in October 1994. Comprising some 40 representatives of most political parties on the island — including the SDLP, Sinn Féin, and the Alliance Party of Northern Ireland — its role is to consult on and examine ways in

58. Former Taoiseach Albert Reynolds (centre), the leader of the SDLP Mr John Hume (right), and the leader of Sinn Féin Mr Gerry Adams.

which lasting peace, stability and reconciliation can be established by agreement among all the people of Ireland. Chaired by Judge Catherine McGuinness, the Forum meets weekly and is seen as having an important contribution to make to the creation of a new era of trust and co-operation on the island. The European Parliament is represented at the Forum in an observer capacity by Mr Leo Tindemans and Mr Piet Dankert.

■ *Framework Document, 1995*
In February 1995 the British and Irish Governments jointly published "A New

59. The US Government has played an important part in advancing the peace process. The picture is of Tánaiste Dick Spring in discussion with President Clinton and Vice-President Gore.

Framework for Agreement", to assist discussion and negotiation involving the Northern Ireland parties. This sets out a shared understanding of the two Governments on how an honourable accommodation could be envisaged across all the relationships, without compromising the long-term aspirations or interests of either tradition or of either community in Northern Ireland.

The document seeks to apply the principles in the Joint Declaration. It sketches out proposals for balanced constitutional change on both sides, and for new structures within Northern Ireland, between North and South and between the two islands. It also envisages enhanced protection for human rights. Proposals for structures within Northern Ireland were developed in a separate British paper "A Framework for Accountable Government in Northern Ireland", published simultaneously with the framework document.

The document was welcomed by the public in both jurisdictions, with the exception of unionist political leaders, who rejected it as a basis for discussion. However successive opinion polls confirm that there is strong support throughout Northern Ireland, including amongst the unionist electorate, for engaging in negotiations, and both Governments will be making determined efforts, in dialogue with the parties, to advance this objective.

Parliamentary Representation

Seventeen MPs from Northern Ireland sit at the United Kingdom Parliament at Westminster. A Boundary Commission report in early 1995 recommended an increase in the number of MPs to eighteen. Northern Ireland elects three Members of the European Parliament. At present the MEPs are Dr. Ian Paisley (Democratic Unionist Party), Mr John Hume (Social Democratic and Labour Party) and Mr. Jim Nicholson (Ulster Unionist Party).

Under the Northern Ireland Act, 1974, the Government of Northern Ireland is exercised through a Secretary of State, appointed by the British Government, who retains responsibility for constitutional matters, security and law and order, and who exercises a special responsibility in overall social and economic planning. There are six Government Departments: Agriculture, Economic Development, Education, Environment, Finance and Personnel, Health and Social Services. There are twenty-six district councils in Northern Ireland responsible for local services such as sanitary, recreational, social, community and cultural facilities, the promotion of tourism and the enforcement of building regulations. The councils are elected by proportional representation on the basis of the single transferable vote.

Government

■ *Legal System*

The courts in Northern Ireland consist of the superior courts (the Supreme Court) and the inferior courts. The Supreme Court comprises the Court of Appeal and the High Court — both of which have jurisdiction in civil and criminal matters — and the Crown Courts, which have jurisdiction solely in criminal matters. The inferior courts are the County Courts, which have jurisdiction in mostly civil matters, and the Magistrates' Courts, which deal with minor civil and criminal cases. In addition to the appeals procedures within the Northern Ireland courts system, in both civil and criminal cases, a judgment of the Court of Appeal may in certain circumstances be appealed to the House of Lords. In December, 1972 a Commission to consider legal procedures to deal with terrorist activities in Northern Ireland, chaired by Lord Diplock, recommended the establishment of non-jury courts to deal with certain serious offences. These courts, which were set up under the Northern Ireland (Emergency Provisions) Act, 1973 are presided over by a single judge. The decisions of these courts may be appealed to the Court of appeal.

Security Forces

The police force in Northern Ireland, the Royal Ulster Constabulary (RUC), currently consists of some 8,500 members. The force is supported by the RUC Reserve which includes about 3,200 full-time and 1,400 part-time members. Nearly 20,000 British Army personnel, including some 5,000 members of a locally based unit, the Royal Irish Regiment, are also currently stationed in Northern Ireland. It is anticipated that these levels will decrease in the aftermath of the paramilitary ceasefires. It is also likely, as tensions ease, that the size of the police force will be reduced.

The Economy

Northern Ireland's GDP in 1992 was Stg £ 11.571 bn. There have been no separate trade figures for Northern Ireland since 1974 when its trade balance was almost in equilibrium. However, it is clear that there was a sharp deterioration in the balance of trade in the mid-1970's which has persisted to the present day.

Agriculture and Forestry

Northern Ireland's agriculture is based almost entirely on family-owned farms. 57,000 people, or 7% of civilian employment, are actively engaged in work on farms. Despite a very suitable climate and soil type, only 6% of the land area is under forest.

Tourism

In 1993 visitor numbers were estimated at 1.26 m by the Northern Ireland Tourist Board, the highest level ever recorded. Income generated was estimated at Stg £ 173 m. The total number of holiday visitors was 251,000; holiday visitors from the Republic — 110,000 visitors, were the largest group, followed by Great Britain — 60,000 visitors, mainland Europe — 43,000 visitors and North America — 27,000 visitors.

Manufacturing Industry

The total number employed in manufacturing industry declined by 36% between 1973 and 1990. The decline has been particularly steep in foreign-owned plants (53%). Overall employment in manufacturing in July, 1993 was 99,360. The main sectors are engineering, drink and tobacco, and textiles. In 1990 there were 207 externally owned industrial plants in Northern Ireland. The largest source of inward investment was Great Britain with 121 plants. The US followed with 30 plants, the Republic with 25 and the rest of the European Union with 20.

Employment

Unemployment was recorded at 13.5% of the insured workforce in August, 1994. The public service sector, which is large by international standards, accounted for 36.4%

60.   The Shannon-Erne Waterway links the canal and river systems of Northern Ireland with those in the Republic. Its restoration was part-funded by the International fund for Ireland.

of those in employment. The Catholic community continues to suffer from a level of unemployment which is significantly higher than the average. The *Fair Employment Act, 1989* includes provisions relating both to the prohibition of discrimination and the promotion of fair employment in the workforce.

Population

In the 1991 census the population of Northern Ireland was recorded at 1,577,836. The majority of the population were recorded as members of the Protestant denominations. These were, Presbyterians: 336,891; Church of Ireland: 279,280; Methodists: 59,517. Members of 'other denominations' (mainly Protestant) were recorded at 122,448. There were 605,639 Catholics. 59,234 persons were recorded as being of no religion and 114,829 did not state a religious denomination. The Belfast City district council area had a population of 279,237; the City of Derry had 95,381 residents.

Services

Public Expenditure
The budget provision for public expenditure for 1993/94 was Stg £ 7.5 bn. There is a large public sector deficit which is offset by a direct subvention from the British Treasury (estimated in 1994 at approx. Stg £ 3 bn). The main expenditure is on Social Security: Stg £ 2.5 bn; Health and Social Services: Stg £ 1.3 bn; and Education, at Stg £ 1.2 bn.

Health and Social Security
Health and social security services are delivered through four Health and Social Services Boards based on local authority districts.

Newspapers and Periodicals
There are two morning daily newspapers: *The News Letter* and *The Irish News*; one evening daily: *The Belfast Telegraph*, and two Sunday newspapers: *The Sunday World* and *The Sunday Life*. In addition, 39 local newspapers are published, one twice-weekly, the others weekly. A number of periodicals cover business, professional and leisure interests.

Radio and Television
There are ten radio stations: seven are operated by the BBC (Radios 1, 2, 3, 4 and 5, *Radio Ulster* and *Radio Foyle*); together with *Downtown Radio*, Belfast (a commercial radio station operated by the Independent Broadcasting Authority); and two local Belfast stations. Both the BBC and the Independent Broadcasting Authority provide local television services — *BBC Northern Ireland* and *Ulster Television* (UTV).

61. Mount Stewart House and Gardens, Co. Down.

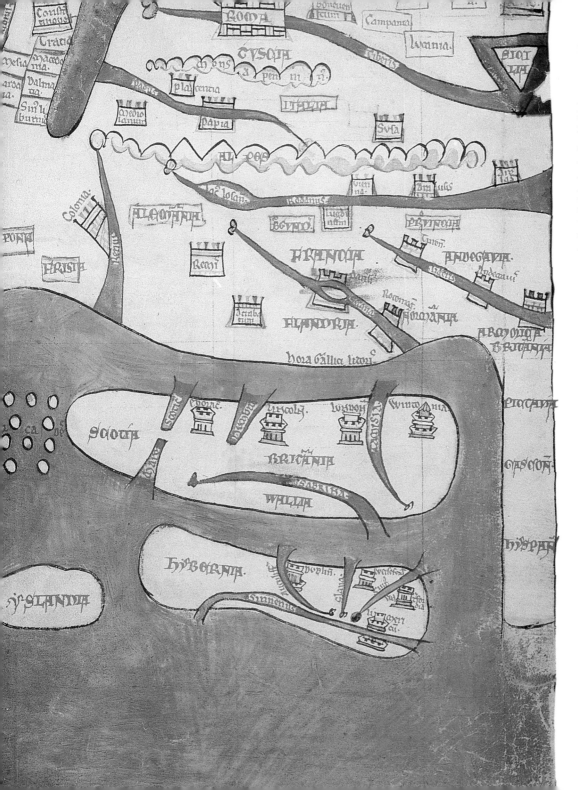

International
Relations

The European
Union

Development
Cooperation

The Irish Abroad

IRISH ONE WORLD QUILT

NATIONAL
WOMENS
FORUM
TRAVELLER

HARMONY

Preceding page:
62. Map of Europe
from the
'Topographia
Hiberniae' (ca AD
1200) by Giraldus
Cambrensis.

International Relations

The Constitution affirms Ireland's devotion to the ideal of peace and friendly cooperation amongst nations founded on international justice and morality. In accordance with the principles set out in the Constitution, foreign policy is based on the conviction that the country's interests, and those of all countries, are best served by respect for the rule of law in international relations. Ireland is committed to the United Nations system and its diplomacy seeks to uphold the values of liberal democracy and, especially, respect for human rights. It has a sense of solidarity with the many countries which also achieved independence only in this century.

Since the early 1800's, Irish people have emigrated in large numbers to many parts of the world. Close economic and cultural ties exist with countries where a significant proportion of the population is of Irish descent. These include Australia, Britain, Canada, New Zealand and the United States.

Diplomatic relations are maintained with 89 countries.

White Paper on Foreign Policy

With a view to encouraging a sense of public ownership of foreign policy, the Government is to publish a White Paper on Foreign Policy in mid-1995. As part of the preparations for the White Paper, a series of open seminars dealing with aspects of foreign policy were held at venues throughout the country in 1994 and early 1995. The topics covered included Development Cooperation, Human Rights, the United Nations and Peace-Keeping, and the European Union and the future evolution of European Security.

The United Nations

Ireland has been a member of the *United Nations* since 1955, and has been active in efforts to maintain international peace and security in accordance with the UN Charter. Ireland has twice served on the Security Council, in 1962 and in 1981–2. The Defence Forces have served with distinction in many UN peace-keeping missions and a significant proportion of their personnel is deployed on UN service today. Members of An Garda Síochána (the police force) have also served in UN peace-keeping operations in recent years (see Police, page 57 and Defence, page 60).

During the plenary debate at the commencement of the General Assembly each year the Minister for Foreign Affairs has traditionally taken the opportunity to outline the Government's approach to global problems and to inform Member States of developments in relation to Northern Ireland.

Ireland supports UN specialised agencies such as the *UN High Commission for Refugees*, the *UN Development Programme*,

64. The Tánaiste (Deputy Prime Minister of Ireland) and Minister for Foreign Affairs, Dick Spring, with the Secretary-General of the United Nations, Boutros Boutros-Ghali.

the *International Labour Organisation* and the *World Health Organisation*. The country plays an active role in the *Commission on Human Rights* and in other UN fora in promoting universal standards of human rights. Ireland has been consistently involved in efforts to promote the limitation of arms, particularly nuclear weapons. The Nuclear Non-Proliferation Treaty originated in an Irish initiative at the UN General Assembly in 1958, and the country was first to ratify the Treaty.

■ *Europe*

In 1949 Ireland was a founder member of the *Council of Europe* which brings together all European parliamentary democracies. Ireland is an active participant in the *Conference on Security and Cooperation in Europe* (CSCE), now renamed the Organisation for Security and Cooperation in Europe (OSCE). The CSCE played an important role in bringing an end to the East — West divide by developing agreed norms and principles governing security, arms control, human rights and cooperation on economic, social and cultural matters. Since the end of the Cold War, the CSCE has evolved into an organisation with a key role in the spread of democratic values and in the promotion of cooperation among all European countries. Ireland is committed to the further development of the OSCE as a pan-European security forum and to achieving a central role for the organisation in continent-wide security arrangements.

■ *Other International Organisations*

The following are some of the other international organisations of which Ireland

is a member: *Bank for International Settlements, European Bank for Reconstruction and Development (EBRD), Food and Agricultural Organisation of the United Nations* (FAO), *International Atomic Energy Agency* (IAEA), *International Bank for Reconstruction and Development* (IBRD, also known as the *World Bank*), *International Civil Aviation Organisation* (ICAO), *International Development Association* (IDA), *International Finance Corporation* (IFC), *International Telecommunications Union* (ITU), *Organisation for Economic Cooperation and Development* (OECD), *United Nations Educational, Scientific and Cultural Organisation* (UNESCO), *Universal Postal Union* (UPU), *World Meteorological Organisation* (WMO) and the *World Trade Organisation* (WTO).

The European Union

On 1 January 1973, Ireland, together with the United Kingdom and Denmark, joined the original six Member States (Belgium, France, Germany, Italy, Luxembourg and the Netherlands) as members of the European Community. (Greece joined in 1981 followed by Spain and Portugal in 1986. Austria, Finland and Sweden became members on 1 January, 1995.)

By the end of 1977, following an initial transition period, all tariffs on trade with other members of the Community had been removed. The Single European Act of 1987 initiated the removal of the remaining barriers to economic activity between Member States. The Single Market was completed on 1 January, 1993.

The European Union was established in November, 1993 on the entry into force of the Treaty of European Union (the

Maastricht Treaty).

Successive Governments have favoured progressive evolution to a closer union. In referenda in 1972, 1987 and 1992 the people overwhelmingly endorsed accession to the Communities and the subsequent treaties involving major steps towards the goal of union.

Ireland nominates one member of the European Commission and elects 15 members to the European Parliament. (There are also 3 members from Northern Ireland.) The country has held the six-month Presidency of the Council of Ministers on four occasions, most recently in 1990, and will do so again during the second half of 1996.

The Single Market: the most obvious economic benefit of membership of the Union has been the unhindered access it allows to a market of some 370 million people. This has in turn required an adjustment of the economy to international competition. Membership has contributed to rapid progress in a range of areas including the development of agriculture, industry and services.

Apart from the economic benefits, membership of the Union has had a major impact on social and cultural life. In addition, every Irish citizen is also an EU citizen. Among the rights conveyed by EU citizenship are the right to move and reside freely within the territory of other Member States, subject to certain limitations.

Economic and social cohesion: the Union embodies the principle of economic and social cohesion according to which the less prosperous regions are helped to reduce

65. The European Parliament, Strasbourg.

disparities between their levels of development and those of the more prosperous regions. This principle was reinforced in the Single European Act and again in the Maastricht Treaty. Under the present round of structural funds, which will apply until the end of 1999, Ireland will receive funding of approximately £1 billion per year.

66. The European Commission, headed by Commission President Jacques Santer.

■ *Economic and Monetary Union*: see chapter on *The Economy* (page 90).

■ *External Relations*
Ireland's membership of the EU is rooted in the understanding that the Union is the cornerstone of political and economic stability in Europe. Apart from the considerable economic and social benefits conferred by the Union, membership enables the country's views and interests to be taken into account in a grouping of major influence in world affairs. Ireland's participation in this grouping enhances its traditional role in promoting a stable, peaceful and prosperous international environment with structures based on the rule of law and respect for human rights and democratic values.

Membership of the Union has strengthened Ireland's contacts with the wider world. In the case of Central and Eastern Europe, the Union and its Member States are committed to developing close economic, political and cultural relations with the countries of the area and to assisting in the process of future integration. Likewise, solid foundations have been laid for closer relations with the Baltic States. Ireland, together with its partners, supports the economic and political reform process in Russia and in the other countries of the former Soviet Union.

The southern and eastern shores of the Mediterranean, as well as the Middle East, are areas with which the Union has strong interests in terms of peace, stability, security and regional economic and social development. In this region, the Union has special relations with Cyprus, Malta and Turkey.

Considerable importance is attached to the Union's relations with the US and Canada. Relations are underpinned by substantial trade and investment flows and by a shared commitment to democracy and human rights. In Latin America, Ireland participates in the development of the Union's relations with such regional entities as the *Mercosur* and *Rio Groups*.

In Asia, mutually beneficial economic and political cooperation is developing with the members of ASEAN (*Association of South East Asian Nations*) and with other countries, many of which are, or are rapidly becoming, major partners in the world trading system.

Development Cooperation: the *European Development Fund* (EDF) is the main financing instrument of the *Lomé Convention*.

Through its participation in the work of the EDF Ireland cooperates in the development of some 70 countries in Africa, the Caribbean and the Pacific.

■ *Common Foreign and Security Policy*
The arrangements for political cooperation between Member States were significantly strengthened by the Maastricht Treaty which provides for the establishment of a *Common Foreign and Security Policy* (CFSP). The CFSP extends and develops political cooperation in several important respects, in particular by setting out objectives for the Union in the international area and by providing for more systematic cooperation and action by Member States. These provisions are intended to strengthen the capacity of the Union to play a constructive role in international affairs through the promotion of peace, stability and prosperity.

The objectives of the Common Foreign and Security Policy include the promotion of international cooperation, the preservation of international peace and security, the development and consolidation of democracy, the rule of law and respect for human rights and fundamental freedoms. These are traditional aims of Ireland's foreign policy. Participation in CFSP enables the country to pursue these aims more effectively, in cooperation with its European partners.

The Maastricht Treaty provides that the Common Foreign and Security Policy shall address all questions relating to the security of the Union, including the eventual framing of a common defence policy which might in time lead to a common defence. It also makes provision for the EU to request the Western European Union (WEU) to elaborate and implement decisions and actions which have defence implications. In view of this relationship between the EU and the WEU, Ireland became an Observer at the WEU on 1 November 1993, the date on which the Maastricht Treaty entered into force.

■ *1996 Intergovernmental Conference*
A conference of the representatives of the Member States of the European Union will be convened in 1996 to examine those provisions of the Treaty for which revision may be required. These provisions include the common foreign and security policy, including the question of a possible common defence policy, the powers of the European Parliament, the size of the European Commission and the system of voting in the council.

Changes in the Treaty's provisions would have to be approved by all Member States and, in the case of Ireland, are likely to require the approval of the people in a referendum.

The Conference will coincide with Ireland's next Presidency of the Union during the second half of 1996.

Development Cooperation

Ireland, recognising that all areas of the world are inter-dependent, acknowledges its obligation to contribute to the economic and social progress of the developing countries.

Private support for Third World causes is extremely high. At about 0.1% of GNP, such support represents one of the highest rates of private development assistance anywhere. In recent years, Irish agencies have played a major role in providing humanitarian assistance in the crises which have arisen in a number of countries. The activities of non-

67. Irish Aid seeks to help the most disadvantaged people in the priority countries. The picture shows President Robinson at a village water supply project during her State visit to Zambia.

Governmental organisations such as *Concern, Trocaire, Goal* and the *Irish Red Cross* have drawn attention to the strength of the public's commitment to the Third World.

■ *Official Development Assistance (ODA)*
Ireland's Official Development Assistance has been expanded significantly in recent years, so as to make steady progress towards the UN goal of 0.7% of GNP. Total expenditure in 1995 is expected to amount to IR£89 million, compared with IR£70 million in 1994. This corresponds to 0.27% of forecast GNP.

The principles underlying development cooperation policy and the priority areas of action for the future were outlined in *A Strategy Plan for Irish Aid: Consolidation and Growth* (1993). The plan provides for the following:

— expenditure on bilateral aid will increase at a faster rate than expenditure on multilateral aid;

— there will be increased funding of development cooperation programmes with individual countries and of emergency relief;

— steady increases will be made in contributions to UN development agencies.

Irish Aid is administered by the *Department of Foreign Affairs* through its Development Cooperation Offices in partner countries. An inter-Departmental committee on development cooperation oversees the programme; a sub-committee approves individual projects. A committee of independent persons advises the Minister for

Foreign Affairs on all matters concerning the development cooperation programme.

■ *Bilateral ODA*
Bilateral assistance includes direct support for development activities in developing countries, the provision of technical assistance, cooperation with non-Governmental organisations, and provision of emergency humanitarian assistance in response to natural or man-made disasters in the developing world. Spending on bilateral assistance is expected to amount to IR£53 million in 1995.

Bilateral cooperation is focused principally on sub-Saharan Africa. Four countries — **Tanzania, Lesotho, Zambia** and **Sudan** have been priority areas for the bilateral aid programme for many years. With the expansion in the resources of the programme the number of priority countries has been extended to include **Ethiopia** and **Uganda**. A development programme is also to be established in **Mozambique**.

The bilateral programme concentrates on achievable objectives within specific geographical regions in these countries. Irish Aid works in cooperation with Governments in partner countries to ensure consistency with their own development strategies. A great deal of emphasis is placed on direct involvement with local communities, and environmental and gender concerns are given a high priority.

Projects in recent years have included, in Lesotho, village water supply and sanitation, technical assistance to the Ministry of Works in Maseru and technical and vocational education. In Tanzania, projects have included rural development at Kilosa, livestock improvement at Pemba and education in hydrology at the University of Dar-Es-Salaam. In Zambia projects have been undertaken at the Dairy Produce Board in Lusaka, on urban renewal and in maternity clinics.

In Sudan, projects have included the provision of water supply for the rural

68. Emergency Seed Distribution Programme, Somalia.

population, forestry planting and primary health care. In Ethiopia, projects include two reconstruction projects and a primary health project. In Uganda, support is given to developing a major district programme in the Kibaale District, a telecommunications project and a UNDP/World Bank research project are also funded.

Other countries in which Ireland operates bilateral ODA programmes include **Somalia** (rehabilitation projects), **Zimbabwe** (agriculture and small business development projects) and **South Africa**, following the transition to non-racial democracy (education, public administration projects). ODA is also provided to **Vietnam** and **Cambodia**, and to the autonomous Palestinian Administration in **Gaza and Jericho**. There is a modest programme of cooperation with the countries of **Eastern and Central Europe**.

■ *Technical Cooperation*
Resources are allocated to technical cooperation, i.e. transfers of technology or skills through the placement of advisers or the provision of fellowships. Advisers may be placed directly by Irish Aid or through the *Agency for Personal Service Overseas* (APSO). The role of advisers is usually aimed at capacity or institution-building.

■ *Emergency Humanitarian Assistance*
Responding to emergencies around the world is an integral part of the ODA programme. Most emergency assistance is channelled through voluntary agencies.

■ *NGO Co-Financing*
Funds are provided to non-Governmental organisations for development projects. In 1993, assistance was provided to 192 projects in 35 countries.

■ *Multilateral ODA*
Multilateral ODA consists largely of contributions to international institutions for use in developing countries. Contributions to the European Union, the United Nations, the World Bank and their related agencies are expected to amount to approximately IR£34 million in 1995.

The largest part of multilateral ODA is channelled through the European Union.

Voluntary contributions are made to UN development and relief agencies. The major recipients in 1995 were the *United Nations Development Programme* (UNDP), the *United Nations International Children's Emergency Fund* (UNICEF) and the *United Nations High Commission for Refugees* (UNHCR).

Contributions are also made to the *World Bank* and to its subsidiary, the *International Development Agency* (IDA). The IDA provides loans on concessionary terms to the least developed countries.

The Irish Abroad

Throughout the early medieval period Irish missionaries preached the gospel and established new monastic communities across the continent of Europe. This first great outward movement in Christian times was halted by the upheavals arising from the Viking impact on Ireland. Much later, with the overthrow of the Gaelic political order by the English in the 17th century, the first major migration of the modern period began.

The social and political disadvantages encountered by the Catholic nobility and gentry encouraged many of them to emigrate to Europe. This exodus reached its peak in the 18th century when Irish soldiers and statesmen earned distinction in the service of many European armies, those of France, Spain and Austria in particular. Thousands of Irishmen, known as the "Wild Geese", whose ranks included names like MacMahon, Taaffe, O'Neill and Butler, died fighting for continental armies up to the time of the Napoleonic wars.

In modern times involvement in the life of continental Europe has been mainly cultural. Joyce and Beckett both deliberately chose the continent as their base. Since acceding to the European Community in 1973 new opportunities to live and work in continental Europe have been created. Increasing numbers of young Irish men and women can now be found in the main EU countries, and this tendency is likely to grow.

■ Great Britain

The pattern of emigration to Britain has changed over the last two centuries. The highest rates occurred during famine years, particularly during the Great Famine from 1846–1851. High rates of emigration were again recorded during the boom years in Britain in the 1950s, which coincided with depression at home. Emigration declined between 1890 and 1935, but then resumed.

It is estimated that there may be up to one million people of Irish birth (including those from Northern Ireland) in Britain today. However, there would be many more second or even third generation Irish, though precise figures are lacking. Many of these are

69. The Irish College at Paris was one of thirty such colleges in Europe. It is today an Irish cultural and educational centre.

■ Continental Europe

From the 16th century onwards the Catholic population suffered substantial religious disabilities. They turned to the Catholic countries of continental Europe for aid and shelter. In 1578 the Irish College was established in Paris to train students for the priesthood. Other colleges were set up at Rome, Louvain, Salamanca and Lisbon.

70. The Irish Post,
founded in 1970,
is a national weekly
in Great Britain.

five million people emigrated in the course of the century. Although the Irish settled all over the United States, they acquired exceptional political influence in cities like Boston, New York, Philadelphia, Chicago and San Francisco. Their highly developed political and organisational skills enabled them achieve control of city administrations and leave a notable mark on the American political style.

Recent statistics indicate that over 40 million persons in the United States claim some Irish ancestry, and that 25% of this figure claim solely Irish ancestry. The States with the largest numbers of Irish-Americans are California, New York and Pennsylvania, in that order. Irish-Americans are found in all areas of political, public, professional and economic life. Complete integration in

conscious of their heritage, and interested in promoting Irish cultural and sporting activities, as could be seen in their contribution to the successes of the Republic of Ireland soccer team.

North America
Movement in appreciable numbers to parts of the world beyond Europe began in the early 18th century. Greater toleration and economic opportunities in the New World attracted many, especially Presbyterians from Ulster. There were large numbers of Irish in the Revolutionary armies. Four signatories of the American Declaration of Independence were of Irish birth, while another nine were of Irish ancestry.

In the early 19th century increasing numbers went to the United States and Canada. The Great Famine hugely accelerated emigration and approximately

71. President
George Washington
presenting Captain
John Barry with his
commission. Barry,
born in 1745 in Co.
Wexford, is popularly
known as the 'father
of the American
navy'.

72. St. Patrick's Day is celebrated by people of Irish origin and by friends of Ireland in the United States and throughout the world. The picture is of Taoiseach (Prime Minister of Ireland) John Bruton with President Clinton and House Speaker Gingrich at a reception hosted by the Speaker at The Capitol, Washington.

American society has not, however, lost all these descendants to the culture and aspirations of Ireland and the maintenance of personal and family links is a continuing aspect of the relationship between the Irish and Irish-American communities.

Many distinguished American politicians are of Irish descent. Recent US Presidents of Irish ancestry included John F. Kennedy, Richard M. Nixon and Ronald Reagan.

Irish immigrants began to arrive in Canada in significant numbers in the 18th and early 19th centuries. By 1867 people of Irish descent comprised over 20% of the Canadian population, being outnumbered only by British and French-Canadians. Many leading figures in Canadian political life in the 19th century were either Irish-born or of Irish descent, including the distinguished statesman Thomas D'Arcy McGee (d. 1868).

More recently, Brian Mulroney has been Prime Minister of Canada.

◼ *Australia*

The Irish have made a significant contribution to the development of Australia and of the Australian identity from the time of the first European settlement there in 1788. Up to 30% of the Australian

73. An Irish language class at the Australian-Irish Summer School.

population is estimated to be of Irish descent, making Australia probably the most 'Irish' country in the world outside of Ireland itself.

In the early years many of those arriving came as convicts, both political and non-political. After the Great Famine increasing numbers of free settlers came, especially from Munster, settling mainly in New South Wales, Victoria and Queensland. These people and their descendants have left a rich legacy in every walk of Australian life, most notably in politics, the trade unions, the churches, education, literature, law, medicine and sport. Their powerful influence on Australian politics is exemplified by the fact that six of the seven Prime Ministers of Australia in the period 1929–49 had Irish forebears. More recently, Prime Minister Paul Keating, who took office in 1991, has relatives in Co. Galway.

In sport, Australian Rules football, the most popular spectator sport in the country, is widely acknowledged as having its origins in Gaelic football. The two codes are so similar that an official international series between Ireland and Australia was inaugurated in 1984 under composite rules.

New Zealand

The Irish presence in New Zealand and their contribution to that country's development has also been considerable. It is estimated that 15% of the total population is of Irish descent. The Irish have played a prominent role in many aspects of New Zealand life. The first premier, John Edward Fitzgerald, was Irish-born. Captain Hobson, who signed the Treaty of Waitangi which founded the modern state of New Zealand, came from Waterford.

Latin America

In the early years of the 19th century, with the end of the wars in Europe, many Irish soldiers went to serve in the armies of the South American republics. At the same time Irish people went to work and farm in South America, especially in Argentina; a high proportion of these came from the Midlands. William Brown, born in Co. Mayo in 1777, arrived in Buenos Aires in 1812 and went on to found the Argentinean navy. Earlier, the Co. Offaly-born Don Ambrosio Higgins served as Spanish viceroy of Peru in the 1700s; his son Bernardo O'Higgins helped secure the independence of Chile and was its first head of government, from 1818 to 1823.

Irishmen also played a notable part in the history of Mexico. In Mexico City today a memorial recalls the Irishmen of the St. Patrick's Battalion who died in the Mexican-American war of 1847.

Epilogue

Ireland has had the highest rate of emigration of any European country for the past two centuries, taking one decade with another. Unusually in the context of European emigration, as many women as men have emigrated. This enabled Irish people to intermarry to a great extent, and thus sustain a lively sense of community abroad. Ireland has also had an exceptionally low rate of return migration. This may now be changing with the growth in the number of educated emigrants during the 1980s. Many of these have gone abroad to gain experience, with the intention of returning if suitable employment opportunities arise. Improved communications also allow for the maintenance of closer and more sustained contact with home.

*Preceding page:
74. Satellite map of
Ireland.*

*This page:
75. Irish business
exports a wide range
of goods. These
include (clockwise
from top left)
pharmaceuticals
manufactured by Leo
Laboratories, data
processing equipment
by Connaught
Electronics,
food, and
fashionwear by
Fisherman Out of
Ireland, Cleo and
Avoca Handweavers.*

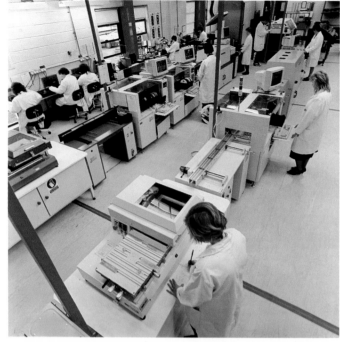

Introduction

The Irish economy is very open. With a domestic market of only 3.5 million people it is heavily dependent on trade; exports of goods and services alone amount to almost 80% of GNP. The rapid pace of development and industrialisation in recent decades has been due in large measure to policies designed to make Ireland an attractive location for overseas investment. As a member of the European Union since 1973, Ireland is part of a large economic area in which goods, services, people and capital can move freely.

The unit of currency is the Irish Pound (IR£ or £).

Figure 5.1

	1988	1989	1990	1991	1992	1993	1994(e)	1995(f)
GNP Volume Growth %	2.3	6.5	9.1	4.6	3.3	3.7	5.5	5.3
Exchequer Borrowing Requirement (*% GNP*)	5.3	2.2	1.9	2.0	2.7	2.4	2.2	2.4
Balance of Payments current account (*% GNP*)	0.3	-1.6	0.2	3.7	5.4	8.6	7.8	7.5

e — estimate; f — forecast

Selected Economic Indicators

In the 1980s policies were implemented to curb imbalances in the public finances. The 1990s have seen the benefit of these policies: the rate of growth in GNP averaged 5.25% per annum in real terms in the years 1988 to 1994. Annual budget deficits fell from over 10 per cent of GNP in 1986 to well under 3% in recent years.

Figure 5.2

£m

Balance of Payments (current account)

(e) = estimate   (f) = forecast

Figure 5.3

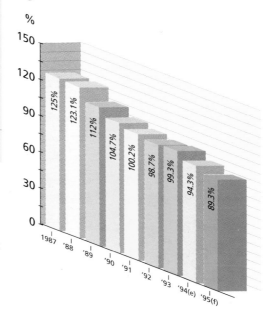

%

125% 123.1% 112% 104.7% 100.2% 98.7% 99.3% 94.3% 89.3%

1987 '88 '89 '90 '91 '92 '93 '94(e) '95(f)

National Debt as a Percentage of GNP

The accumulated debt as a proportion of GDP fell each year, from approximately 112% in 1987 to approximately 90% in 1994, and is forecast to continue falling. The rate of inflation fell from more than 20% in 1981 to well under 3% in recent years. The balance of payments moved from a deficit of IR£650m in 1985 to an estimated surplus of IR£2,420m in 1994. Employment expanded by an average of 9,000 per year in the period 1986–1991, and by 36,000 in 1994.

Living standards have been converging on European levels over the past two decades. This convergence has become more marked in recent years. Per capita GNP rose from approximately 60% of the European average in 1970 to over 70% of the European Union average in 1995.

■ *European Economic and Monetary Union*

Ireland has been a member of the *European Monetary System* since its inception in 1979. The Maastricht Treaty on European Union sets out the steps to full *Economic and Monetary Union*; the final stage, involving the introduction of a single currency, is to begin between 1997 and 1999. The Treaty sets out criteria for participation in the final stage. These include a low level of inflation, a Government deficit of below 3% of GDP, and a ratio of Government debt to GDP of under 60% (or a satisfactory rate of progress in reducing debt to that level).

Ireland has an excellent inflation record in recent years and the Government deficit has been below 3% of GDP every year since 1989. As stated above, steady progress has been made in reducing the level of debt to GDP.

The Government is committed to maintaining the economic discipline necessary to qualify for EMU.

Figure 5.4

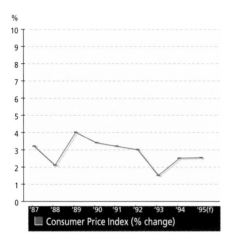

Consumer Price Index (% change)

Figure 5.5

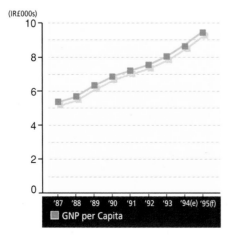

GNP per Capita

Figure 5.6

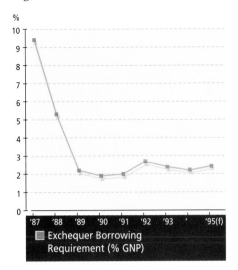

indigenous industry, but by the 1950s these measures were clearly not contributing to economic development. Industry was stagnating and the opportunities for expanding employment through dependence on the home market had become limited.

Ireland's industrial breakthrough had its roots in decisions taken in the 1950's to achieve economic expansion by stimulating export-based industrial development.

In 1952 Córas Tráchtála, the Irish Export Board, was established to promote exports and in the same year the first capital incentive schemes were introduced to encourage the establishment of new industry in underdeveloped areas. In 1958 the first tax incentives were introduced to encourage the expansion of industrial exports. The Industrial Development Authority was given the role of promoting industry with a mandate to assist the indigenous sector and to encourage foreign firms to set up new industries.

The Anglo-Irish Free Trade Agreement in 1965 contributed to the opening-up of the

When the modern Irish State was founded in 1922 the industrial sector was made up of a small number of manufacturers, largely in traditional sectors — food, drink, textiles — producing almost exclusively for the home market.

Protectionist measures were introduced in the 1930s to encourage the expansion of

76. Olympus (IRL) Ltd. manufacture diagnostic equipment for the healthcare industry at O'Callaghan's Mills, Co. Clare.

Irish economy. Accession to the EEC in 1973 brought tariff-free access to the markets of the Community for Irish goods. In the early 1970s the Industrial Development Authority encouraged industry in export-oriented growth sectors such as electronics, engineering and pharmaceuticals to set up in Ireland. These developments fostered a much more open economy and a strong growth in exports. Exports of goods and services amounted to 37% of GNP in 1973; these rose to 56% in 1983 and to 79% in 1994.

The increased pace of economic development since the 1960s has been accompanied by significant changes in the composition of output and employment. In 1995 industry (including construction) accounted for about 28% of total employment compared to 21% in 1949, while agriculture represented 11% of total employment, compared to 43% in 1949. As in other countries, the share of the agricultural sector in employment has been falling steadily while that of services has been rising.

Figure 5.7

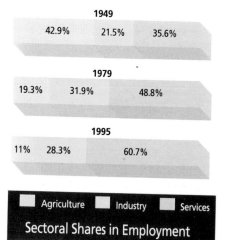

1949

42.9% 21.5% 35.6%

1979

19.3% 31.9% 48.8%

1995

11% 28.3% 60.7%

■ Agriculture ■ Industry ■ Services

Sectoral Shares in Employment

In the mid-1980s the economy faced a number of serious difficulties, the most important of which were declining employment, substantial emigration and a rapidly rising national debt. To deal with these problems, the Government, employers and trade unions agreed in 1987 on a three-year *Programme for National Recovery*. This emphasised fiscal and monetary stabilisation, tax reform, pay moderation and sectoral development on the basis of consensus. The programme proved successful and was followed by two others: the *Programme for Economic and Social Progress* (1991 to 1993) and the *Programme for Competitiveness and Work* which began in 1994.

As a result of these programmes economic growth has been over twice the EU average, inflation has fallen to one of the lowest rates in the EU, and employment in the private non-agricultural sector has shown an annual average growth of about 2.5%. Budgetary consolidation measures linked to the programmes have given Ireland one of the lowest Government deficits in the EU.

New industrial promotion agencies were established in 1994: Forbairt has responsibility for indigenous industry, IDA-Ireland is charged with attracting investment from abroad. Shannon Development (or SFADCO – the Shannon Free Airport Development Company) and Udarás na Gaeltachta (authority for Irish-speaking areas) promote investment in the particular regions for which they are responsible. Forfás (the policy and advisory board for industrial development) has a coordinating role amongst these and other agencies.

Through these agencies a very significant and generous programme of incentives is made available, mainly in the form of cash grants and tax reliefs. These, together with a progressive business climate and a well-educated and productive labour-force, have made Ireland a highly profitable location for industrial investment.

◼ *Structural and Cohesion Funds*
Competitiveness and opportunities for productive investment are being boosted by the further development of economic infrastructure. Real economic convergence within the EU is being assisted by Structural and Cohesion Funds for qualifying regions, including Ireland, over the period 1994 to 1999. Overall, total investment of around IR£20 billion will be put in place, funded by the EU and by matching public and private sector investment. This investment will improve the country's growth potential through a major up-grading of physical infrastructure, the development of indigenous industry, natural resources and tourism and the improvement of training and employment skills.

Labour Force

The population of the State in 1994 was estimated at 3.571 million. Approximately 43% of the population is under 25 and the proportion of working age (15 to 64 years) is 63%.

In 1994 the total labour force was estimated at 1.397 million. At 39% of the total population this is significantly lower than the European Union average of approximately 43%. The disparity between the Irish and European figures arises from the large proportion of young people and the relatively small number of women in the labour force.

Figure 5.8

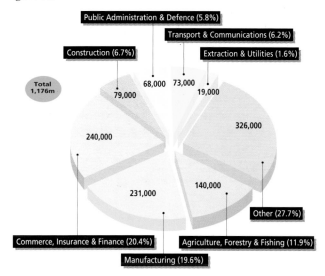

Estimated Employment by Main Branches of Activity, 1994

◼ *Unemployment*
At about 14 % of the labour force, the unemployment rate is among the highest in the OECD. However, the gap between Irish unemployment and that for the rest of Europe narrowed during the recession of the early 1990's as employment in Ireland continued to expand while it fell elsewhere.

This expansion was underpinned by strong economic growth despite the severe international recession. The economy is well-positioned to benefit from the recovery in the European economy over the coming years. This should lead to faster employment growth and lower unemployment. However, given the large potential increase in the labour force, a high rate of employment growth is needed to reduce unemployment. In the absence of emigration the labour force is expected to increase by approximately

1.7% per annum until the end of the decade. Furthermore, the proportion of the population of working age in the labour force is expected to increase as more married women take up employment. In addition to the general problem of unemployment there are the particular problems of large numbers of long-term and youth unemployed. The number of people without employment for more than a year is close to half of the registered total. Close to 30 per cent of the unemployed are under 25 years of age, although this age group represents only 20%, approximately, of the total labour force.

Agriculture

Despite the gradual decline in the relative importance of agriculture in the past few decades the sector still remains one of the most important indigenous industries in the country. Agriculture accounts for 8.1% of GDP, 13.8% of employment and (food and agricultural products) for 21% of exports (1993). This compares with an EU average of 2.8% of GDP, 5.8% of employment and 8.9% of exports.

There are approximately 170,000 farms and the average size is 26 hectares; the vast majority are owned and operated by farming families. When those engaged in agriculture-related industries, particularly food-processing, are included the contribution of the sector to overall employment is about 16%. Further employment is provided in service industries, particularly in those towns servicing the agricultural hinterland. There has been a fairly rapid decrease in agricultural employment as productivity has increased, and output has grown due to the application of modern techniques and practices in the industry.

Over half the value of agricultural production is exported. However, for cattle and beef production the export proportion is higher, with over 80% of production going abroad. An increasing proportion of agricultural output undergoes processing before export. For example, live exports of cattle now account for approximately 16% of cattle and beef exports, compared to over 60% in the mid-1960s.

77. Ireland's climate and soil are ideal for livestock raising.

The land tenure system is one of owner occupation — the great majority of farms are run by farmers themselves with some help from their families. The primary aim of land policy is to ensure that agricultural land is, as far as practicable, in the management or ownership of those best fitted to work it to optimum national advantage. A complementary aim is the improvement of the physical structure of agricultural holdings. At 26 hectares the average holding is comparable to holdings in most other EU Member States. Farms tend to be larger on the better land in the east and south of the country.

Figure 5.9

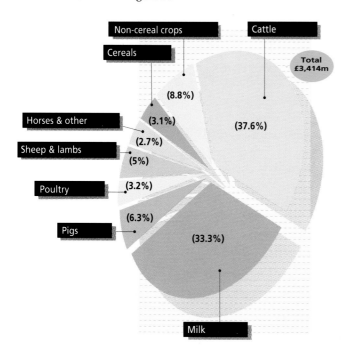

Gross Agricultural Output, 1994

With mild temperatures and relatively high rainfall, conditions are ideally suited to stock raising, with the result that livestock husbandry dominates agricultural production. In 1994 the cattle population stood at 7.08 million including over 2.3 million cows. Almost 90% of the value of gross output is accounted for by livestock and livestock products, almost all of which derive from cattle and milk. Pigs, sheep and lambs account for most of the remainder. Conditions are also suitable for the production of crops. Barley, wheat, sugar beet and potatoes represent an important source of farm income.

Forests occupy 550,000 hectares or almost 8% of the land area. In 1920 less than 1% of the country was under woodland. The development of forestry was taken up by the State and has been intensified since the 1950s. Annual planting rates have increased from 400 hectares in the early years to 23,000 hectares in 1994 and the planting of 30,000 hectares per annum is expected by 1996. Eighty per cent of the forest estate is in public ownership. Planting by the private sector, however, has increased substantially in recent years. **Coillte Teoranta** (the Irish Forestry Board), established in 1988, manages the commercial aspects of the State's forest estate. The promotion of private sector forestry remains the responsibility of the Forest Service of the Department of Agriculture, Food and Forestry. The continuous development and expansion of this sector is encouraged through grant assistance and technical advice. The sector has attracted the interest of farmers, financial institutions and private

Forestry

individuals. A record total of 13,000 hectares was planted by the private sector in 1994, a figure which is expected to increase in years to come.

While the proportion of land area covered by forests is low, the planting rate is the highest per capita forest planting programme of any developed country. Ireland has a combination of soils and a moist mild climate which makes it particularly suitable for growing conifers. Being an island, the country enjoys relative isolation from pests and disease and this contributes to a healthy environment for growing trees.

The ancient native forests of Ireland were mainly of oak, mixed with some ash and elm. Scots pine and birch grew on poorer soils and there were scrub woodlands of alder and willow on marshy ground near lakes and rivers. The emphasis in the new forest has changed from predominantly European species to coniferous species such as Sitka spruce and lodgepole pine from the western part of North America. While these species today comprise nearly 90% of planting, the proportion of broadleaves being planted is increasing.

As the high level of planting dates only from the 1950s and as crops take about 45 years to mature, the output of the forest estate has yet to reach its full potential. Forecasts are that annual wood production will rise from 2.1 million cubic metres in 1994 to 3 million cubic metres by the year 2000. Mature trees are used by the saw-milling industry for construction timber, while small diameter wood (pulpwood), mainly a product of thinnings, is used as a raw material for chipboard, fibreboard, boxwood and fencing. Virtually all available

78. *Timber for export, Cork Harbour.*

supplies are utilised by the medium density fibreboard plant at Clonmel, Co Tipperary and by the chipboard plant at Scariff, Co Clare. A new oriented strand board plant is scheduled to commence production in Waterford in 1995 and in the following year a masonite plant is to open in Carrick-on-Shannon. Forest-based employment could rise to 13,000 by the end of the century.

Coillte Teoranta operates an "open forest" policy which provides public access facilities ranging from picnic stops to nature trails to forest parks with holiday facilities.

Fisheries

The main varieties of sea fish landed are herring, cod, whiting, mackerel, plaice, ray, skate and haddock. Among shellfish, lobsters, periwinkles, crayfish and oysters are taken. In 1994 the total value of the catch

79. *Supertrawler —
MFV Veronica.*

excluding salmon landed by Irish registered vessels in Irish ports was IR£109 million, while exports of fish and fish products were valued at IR£180 million. Approximately 7,700 full-time and part-time fishermen are employed in the industry.

Bord Iascaigh Mhara (Sea Fisheries Board – BIM) is the State body with primary responsibility for the development of the sea fishing and aquaculture industries. BIM provides financial, technical, educational, resource development and marketing services to the catching and aquaculture sectors through to the processing and marketing sectors.

The country's fresh and salt water sport fisheries form a natural resource with considerable potential for development, particularly in the area of angling tourism. The greatest concentration of coarse angling is on the Shannon and Erne river systems, with some smaller fisheries being developed in the West and South. Tourist anglers

seeking salmon fish mainly in the rivers and lakes along the west and south coasts, while brown trout fishing is popular on the large Western lakes and on the smaller Midland lakes.

In 1994 one in twenty of all overseas visitors to the country engaged in angling and these 204,000 people contributed approximately IR£57 million to the economy. Over 50% of visiting anglers fished for coarse fish, but game (particularly trout) and sea angling is more popular with Irish anglers.

■ *Aquaculture*
Ireland's coastal waters are ideally suited for aquaculture. The country's extensive estuaries and coastal areas can support a thriving industry many times larger than exists at present.

Aquaculture provides sustainable additional employment and income in remote and disadvantaged areas. From a negligible level in the mid-1980s the industry has grown to the point where some 2,600 people were engaged in it on a full or part-time basis in 1993. Further employment is provided in feed and equipment manufacture and in processing. The value of aquaculture output was estimated at IR£51 million in 1993, amounting to over 25% of the value of all primary fish production. Output is targeted to increase to IR£103 million by 1999.

Farmed salmon accounted for over 80% of the value of aquaculture output during 1993. The aquaculture development programme to 1999 sees the expansion of shellfish farming as a key element, placing particular emphasis on expanding the production of mussels, oysters, scallops, abalone and other novel species.

Industry

The small amount of industry at independence in 1922 was highly concentrated in Dublin and the main ports. Major initiatives were taken in industrial policy in the early 1960s. As well as creating an investment climate to encourage export-oriented companies to establish in Ireland, a concerted effort was made to spread the benefits of industrialisation to all parts of the country. Preferential incentives were given to firms willing to locate in less developed regions. There is now a wide spread of industry in cities and towns throughout the country.

Membership of the European Community in 1973 increased the attractions of Ireland as a base for manufacturing industry, while at the same time presenting new challenges to existing industry.

The most significant feature of the evolution of employment in manufacturing industry has been the rise in employment in the metals and engineering sector from 21,100 in 1958 to almost 70,000 in 1994. Similar rates of increase have occurred in employment in the minerals and chemicals sectors. In the same period the sectors which showed the greatest decline were clothing and footwear and textiles. The contribution of these traditional labour intensive industries had declined from 19.2% in 1958 to 10% in 1994.

An intensive campaign in the 1960s to attract foreign industry prevented the loss of skills that might have disappeared with the collapse of the traditional industries which had been established during the period of protectionism. The 1970s were to see a more selective approach to attracting foreign investment. This involved targeting key overseas sectors producing sophisticated and high value products which would offer the best growth potential. The sectors chosen were the chemicals and pharmaceutical industry, the electronics industry, and more recently the international traded services sector.

The chemical, pharmaceutical and health care sectors hardly existed in Ireland prior to 1970 but after 1972 they grew by over 40% annually. In recent years the average growth rate of the pharmaceuticals industry (1985–1993) has been a healthy 13%. Sixteen of the world's top twenty ranked chemicals and pharmaceutical companies now manufacture in Ireland. The country has become the world's 15th largest exporter of these products which comprise 18.6% of total exports. The main products are fine chemicals, drugs and hospital products,

Facing page: 80. Pratt and Whitney (IRL) Ltd re-manufacture jet engine casings at Rathcoole in Co. Dublin.

SHW-CNC

81. *Irish exporters of services participate also in EU programmes to assist the new democracies in Eastern Europe. The picture is of a trade development workshop in Slovakia, managed by TDI.*

medical equipment, cosmetics and toiletries. There is increasing emphasis on Research and Development.

■ *Electronics/Software/Telemarketing*
More than 300 of the world's leading electronics companies have invested in Ireland. The electronics industry has come a long way since final assembly was the norm; today many of the leading multinationals such as Analog Devices, Phillips, Northern Telecom, Dell, Gateway, SCI Instruments, Motorola, to name a few, undertake complex manufacturing and development activity from their Irish base. The electronics industry gives direct employment to over 30,000 people and provides numerous sub-contract and indirect employment opportunities. It exports in excess of

IR£4,500m or, on average, 25% of total exports.

The software industry is ideally suited to Ireland. It is labour- rather than capital-intensive and demands highly-skilled young people. It has no undesirable environmental side-effects. The sector comprises over 400 companies (80 from overseas) employing nearly 9,000 people. It is estimated that the industry can grow to employ 20,000 by the end of the decade.

Telemarketing developed rapidly in the first half of the 1990s. It has only two raw materials: quality personnel and sophisticated telecommunications. Both are readily available in Ireland. A IR£2 billion telecommunications programme to provide one of the most modern networks in Europe has recently been completed. There is a ready availability of skilled people with the required languages and large numbers of highly qualified software and technical graduates are produced every year. Telecommunications charges have been rebalanced in order to favour international business. There are already over 500 employed in this sector and this number is expected to increase to 2,000 by 1997.

Financial incentives for foreign investors are administered by IDA-Ireland. They include:

- a reduced corporation tax rate of 10% on profits from manufacturing and international services;
- generous capital allowances for tax purposes;
- cash grants towards fixed assets up to a maximum of 60% depending on the location, size and nature of the project;
- staff training grants of up to 100% for workers in new industries.

IDA-Ireland maintain offices in Europe, the United States and the Far East, the Middle East and Australia.

Over 1,000 foreign firms have set up manufacturing bases in Ireland. Apart from generating almost 100,000 direct jobs in industry their net contribution to the economy each year is approximately IR£3,000m. The country's strong export performance is also strongly influenced by overseas companies. Approximately 55% of manufactured output and 76% of manufactured exports are attributed to overseas owned industry.

Figure 5.10

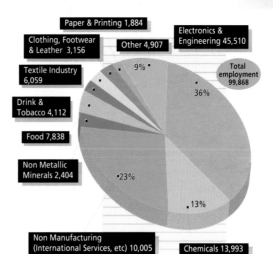

Overseas Companies by sector, 1995
(% of total companies)

Figure 5.11

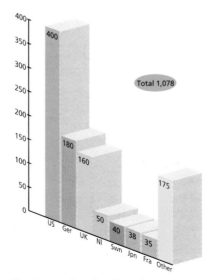

Number and nationality of overseas companies in Ireland, 1995

82. Kromberg and Schumbert (IRL) Ltd., manufacture cable harnesses and leads for the automotive industry at Waterford.

The Government is committed to creating an environment conducive to industrial development and risktaking, and to the achievement of greater efficiency in the industrial incentives available. In addition to attracting foreign investment, special emphasis is being placed on developing strong indigenous companies. There has been a switch from incentives for fixed asset investment towards marketing and technology acquisition. Special emphasis has been placed on encouraging domestically controlled companies to acquire greater competitiveness internationally. Irish controlled companies are also encouraged to address the substantial supply requirements of large-scale industry at home. Other areas focused on are the computer and financial service sectors which are expected to grow

over the coming years. Overseas companies are now obtaining the essential ingredient for this knowledge-intensive sector, namely highly-skilled human resources, in Ireland.

Because of its small size, the economy is highly dependent on foreign trade. A population of approximately 3.5 million offers limited possibilities for industrial expansion based on the domestic market. Moreover, a lack of resources necessitates the importation of large quantities of fuels, raw materials and other basic requirements.

Traditional manufactures (processed foods, drink, clothing, fabrics, handicrafts, etc.) continue as important export items. But it is industrial products (chemicals and pharmaceuticals, automatic data-processing equipment, electrical machinery, scientific instruments, telecommunications equipment, synthetic fibres and the like) which account, by value, for the bulk of manufactured exports and are the mainspring for overall expansion. These products currently account for approximately two-thirds of total exports by value compared with one-quarter in the early 1960s.

The two main sources of exports are (i) an extensive and still-growing manufacturing sector featuring some of the world's latest high-technology developments as well as new and traditional consumer requirements and (ii) a large agricultural and agriculture-based sector with a high degree of emphasis on meat and dairy products. In any representative list of Irish exports, items such as computers, software, radar protection apparatus, industrial sealants, rock-drilling equipment and container cranes will be

Foreign Trade

Figure 5.12

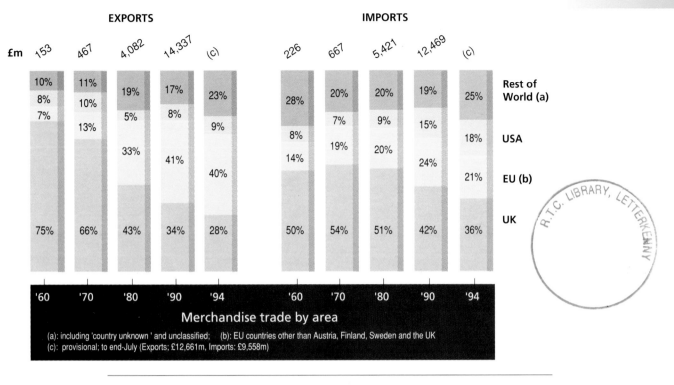

Merchandise trade by area

(a): including 'country unknown' and unclassified;   (b): EU countries other than Austria, Finland, Sweden and the UK
(c): provisional; to end-July (Exports; £12,661m, Imports: £9,558m)

Figure 5.13

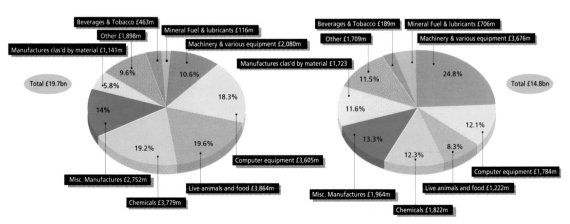

Composition of Exports and Imports, 1993

found side by side with beef, butter, tweeds, fashion, glassware, whiskey, cattle and horses.

Apart from merchandise exports, an important and growing contribution to export activity has come from firms providing services in various fields. One of the most important service sectors is construction-related consultancy, which includes architecture, engineering and quantity surveying. There are strong indications of further progress in this and other service sectors, including power generation, aviation, agricultural development and processing, health, general consultancy, education and training.

The value of exports to the United Kingdom has continued to increase, but the proportion of total exports to that market has declined substantially due to a faster rate of increase in sales elsewhere, most notably to the other members of the European Union. Significant expansion has also taken place in North America and in newer markets such as the Middle East, North Africa, Australia and the Far East.

Merchandise exports amounted to IR£19.7 billion in 1993 corresponding to 68% of GNP, a very high proportion by international standards. This represented an increase over the 1992 figure of approximately 18% by value. The manufactured goods sector accounts for over two-thirds of total exports. Principal export markets in 1993 were: the **UK** (IR£5.6 billion), **Germany** (IR£2.6 billion), the **USA** (IR£1.8 billion), **France** (IR£1.8 billion), and **the Netherlands** (IR£1.1 billion).

The value of exports has exceeded imports for several years. The trade surplus

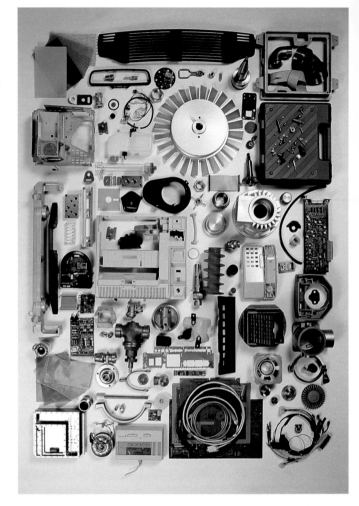

was IR£4.9 billion in 1993. The import bill is mainly accounted for by industrial demand for capital equipment, goods for further processing, raw materials and fuels; these, in the aggregate, make up some 75% of total imports by value.

The UK is the main source of imports, providing up to 36% of the total in 1993. As in the case of exports, the percentage of imports coming from the UK is falling over the long term as trade with other areas

83. A range of electrical and machine components are manufactured in Ireland.

expands. The EU (excluding the UK) ranks second as a provider of imports (20%), and the USA third (17%). Total imports in 1993 were valued at IR£14.8 billion.

An Bord Tráchtála (the Irish Trade Board), is the State organisation with responsibility for the promotion and development of exports. Through its network of 23 overseas offices and 6 regional offices at home, the agency establishes links between Irish companies and prospective clients by identifying opportunities, developing contacts and thus assisting firms to build markets both at home and overseas.

Mineral Resources Ireland is a major mineral producer and is

regarded as one of the most promising exploration territories in Europe. Base-metal exploration over the past thirty years has led to many discoveries, particularly of zinc-lead (Ireland is the largest European producer of this commodity). Recent work has also confirmed the country's potential for gold deposits, while significant deposits of a variety of industrial minerals are known to occur, including gypsum, talc, calcite, dolomite, roofing slate, limestone, aggregate, building stone, and sand and gravel. There are limited resources of coal, although there are still significant reserves of peat which is used both for electricity generation and for domestic and industrial heating.

84. Tara Mines, Co. Meath, exploits Europe's largest deposit of zinc and lead.

Figure 5.14

DEPOSIT	RESERVES (Millions of Tonnes)	GRADE (Zinc and Lead)
Navan, Co Meath	40.00 Mt	9.76%
Galmoy, Co Kilkenny	6.18 Mt	12.43%
Lisheen, Co Tipperary	22.30 Mt	13.9%

Base Metal Deposits

Energy

■ *Hydrocarbon Exploration*

Exploration for oil and gas began in the early 1960s. The emphasis in the early days was on onshore basins. Offshore exploration began in 1970, leading to the discovery of the Kinsale Head Gas Field in 1971 and the smaller Ballycotton Gas Field in 1989. Gas is now piped ashore from these fields. In addition, a number of sub-commercial discoveries of oil and gas have been made. In all, 118 exploration and appraisal wells have been drilled offshore.

The introduction of two major initiatives in 1992 involving taxation incentives and the revision of licensing terms has contributed towards a significant rise in interest in offshore exploration, involving the participation of many of the major exploration companies. Continuing developments in deep sea technologies has also opened up possibilities in the deep water areas off the West coast. The combination of the tax changes and the licensing terms has placed Ireland in a very competitive position for attracting exploration investment.

Government responsibility for hydrocarbon exploration and development is exercised by the Department of Transport, Energy and Communications.

■ *Gas*

Bord Gáis Eireann (Irish Gas Board — BGE) was established by the State in 1976 to develop and maintain a system of supply of natural gas to the domestic energy markets. As its first step in supplying natural gas, Bord Gáis undertook the provision of the onshore pipeline from the Kinsale Head gas field and the associated facilities necessary for distribution of gas to users in the Cork area, including electricity generating plants, local industry and domestic consumers.

The construction in 1982 of the 220 km Cork-Dublin pipeline made natural gas available to the Dublin market. The network now extends from Cork, via Carlow and Dublin, to Dundalk, with a westward spur to Counties Louth and Cavan. Limerick City has also been connected to the gas grid. Approximately 210,000 customers in the industrial, commercial and domestic sectors are supplied with natural gas.

As existing reserves (Kinsale Head and the smaller Ballycotton Field) will be depleted early in the next decade, a gas interconnector pipeline linking the UK grid in Scotland with the Irish grid at Ballough in North Co. Dublin has been constructed. The pipeline will be used initially to access alternative emergency supplies in the event of a disruption in supply from the Kinsale Head platforms and to augment production as the fields decline. When indigenous supplies are exhausted, the pipeline will be used to import gas from the North Sea.

■ *Electricity*

The *Electricity Supply Board* (ESB) was established by the State in 1927 with responsibility for the generation and

Facing page: 85. The upper and lower lakes of the ESB's pumped storage power station, Turlough Hill, Co Wicklow.

distribution of electricity. The ESB has approximately 1.35 million consumers throughout the country.

The domestic distribution system operates at 220 volts/50 cycles. Electricity output in 1994 was some 16,420 million units. Domestic demand represented about 38% of sales; the balance was used by industry and commerce.

With the commissioning of the last of three 300 megawatt units of coal fired plant at Moneypoint in the Shannon Estuary in 1987 the ESB completed the process of switching its base load to coal fired plant. Coal, with the help of indigenous natural gas, has reduced the ESB's dependence on oil from 70% in 1979 to about 17% in 1994. In 1994 coal accounted for about 40% of electricity produced, peat for 11%, gas for 26% and hydro for 6%.

The ESB has established a number of wholly owned subsidiary companies including *ESB International Ltd.* which was set up to develop the company's consultancy business at home and abroad.

▪ *Turf/Peat*

While Ireland lacks sizeable coal deposits, it has a valuable energy source in the peat or turf bogs which cover extensive areas of the country. Turf has been an invaluable source of energy for generations. Turf as a fuel assumed a new dimension with the establishment in 1946 of *Bord na Móna* (Peat Development Board), a State company. Peat production is a major industry and its contribution to security of energy supply has been demonstrated many times against a backdrop of uncertainty on the world's energy scene.

At present, *Bord na Móna's* annual contribution to national requirements is of the order of 813,000 tonnes of oil equivalent. Most of the peat produced is used to generate electricity. In the solid fuel sector both machine turf and peat briquettes make a valuable contribution. Moss peat is extensively used by the horticulture sector and a large export market has been developed.

The Board's engineers have developed sophisticated machinery to harvest peat from bogs and have placed the country at the forefront of peat technology. In 1994, the Board employed about 2,270 workers and produced over 4 million tonnes of peat together with 1.1. million cubic metres of moss peat.

Figure 5.15

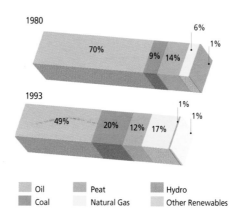

1980

70% 9% 14% 6% 1%

1993

49% 20% 12% 17% 1% 1%

Oil   Peat   Hydro
Coal   Natural Gas   Other Renewables

Total Primary Energy Requirement, 1980 and 1993

▪ *Oil Supplies*

Ireland's only oil refinery is the hydro-skimming unit at Whitegate, Co. Cork.

Whitegate has a capacity of 50,000 barrels per day and is owned by the State oil company, *Irish National Petroleum Corporation*. Its current rate of production is around 43,200 barrels per day which represents about 39% of the country's oil product requirement.

■ *Renewable Energy Sources*

The development of indigenous energy resources is vital in view of the predominant dependence on imported fuels for the country's energy requirements. The increased use of new and alternative sources of energy holds enormous potential for the future. Renewable energy technologies include solar, wind, biomass, water and geothermal energy.

Renewable sources currently provide about 2% of the country's energy requirement. The biggest contributors to renewable services are the ESB hydro-electric schemes and Biomass, particularly wood.

Because of their scattered nature, renewables are particularly suitable for regional applications.

The regions with high levels of exploitable potential are often areas with relatively low levels of economic activity. An example is Bellacorick, Co Mayo where Ireland's first wind farm is located. This was commissioned in October, 1992 and was partly funded by the *EU VALOREN Programme*. It is now the largest single private source of supply to the ESB and has demonstrated the potential which exists for wind power.

Private hydro-sources contribute a modest 8 MWs of capacity and there are some 60 MWs of Combined Heat and Power (CHP) capacity in the country at present. To set this in context, the ESB have 4,000 MWs of installed capacity overall.

The Government launched an initiative in 1993 to achieve further supplies from alternative energy sources. The target is an additional 75MW's of installed capacity before 1997 from independent sources. The scheme is expected to bring wind generating capacity of up to 30 MWs into operation, additional combined heat and power capacity of up to 20 MWs, up to 10 MWs of hydro projects and up to 15 MWs from other alternative sources.

Industrial Relations

Trade unionism first emerged in the larger cities (Dublin, Belfast and Cork) during the 18th century, despite legislation against combinations of workers.

The first association of trade unions, representing thirty crafts and industries, was formed in 1863 and in 1894 the Irish Trades Union Congress, representing most Irish and British unions in the country, was established. *The Irish Congress of Trade Unions* (ICTU), established in 1959, is now the main co-ordinating body of Irish unions and includes unions in Northern Ireland. At the end of 1994 there were 58 trade unions in the State representing some 490,000 workers. About 50% of all employees are union members.

The *Services, Industrial, Professional and Technical Union* (SIPTU), formed in 1990 through the amalgamation of the Irish Transport and General Workers Union and the Federated Workers Union of Ireland, is the largest trade union with 202,000 members in the Republic. Other large unions are the *Irish Municipal Public and Civil Trade Union* (28,000 members), the

86. Biannual conference of the Irish Congress of Trade Unions.

Technical Engineering and Electrical Union (23,000 members), the *Manufacturing, Science and Finance Union* — UK based — (21,000 members) and the *Irish National Teachers Organisation* (20,000 members).

The main representative organisation of the management side of industry and business is the *Irish Business and Employers Confederation* (IBEC). There are a number of other employers' associations organised on a sectoral or regional basis.

The Constitution guarantees the right of citizens to form associations and unions while the State is allowed to enact legislation for the regulation and control of this right in the public interest. Legislation gives immunity from civil legal proceedings to acts done in contemplation of furtherance of a trade dispute. This immunity is confined to trade unions holding negotiation licences from the Minister for Enterprise and Employment. The Minister grants a licence once certain legal conditions are met, the

most important of which are the maintenance of a substantial deposit of money in the High Court and a minimum level of membership.

The industrial relations system is voluntary. Pay and conditions of employment are generally agreed through free collective bargaining between employers and employees, although for some occupations there are statutory minimum pay scales. While certain basic rights covering such matters as minimum notice, dismissal, holidays, redundancy payments and employment equality are provided for in legislation, involvement by the State in industrial relations is in the main confined to the provision of machinery to assist the parties to a dispute to find a solution.

The principal mediation bodies are the *Labour Relations Commission* and the *Labour Court*. The *Labour Relations Commission*, which comprises equal numbers of employer and trade union representatives as well as independent representatives, was set up under the Industrial Relations Act, 1990. The Commission has general responsibility for the promotion of good industrial relations through the provision of a comprehensive range of services to help prevent and resolve disputes. The Commission's Conciliation Service helps employers and workers and their trade unions to resolve disputes where direct negotiations under collective bargaining have failed.

The *Labour Court*, established under the Industrial Relations Act, 1946, consists of a chairperson, deputy chairpersons and ordinary members representative of employers and workers. The Court normally investigates disputes only if either (i) it receives a report from the Labour Relations Commission that no further efforts on its part will help resolve the dispute or (ii) the Commission waives its function of conciliation in the dispute. The Court, having investigated a dispute, usually issues a recommendation giving its opinions on the merits of the dispute and the terms on which it should be settled. Except in certain cases, the Court's recommendations are not legally binding.

For a limited number of industries and trades **Joint Labour Committees**, which draw up minimum rates of pay and other conditions of employment, operate. These rates become legally binding when ratified by the Labour Court in the form of **Employment Regulation Orders**. Another minimum pay enforcement procedure arises when the Court registers an employment agreement. A Registered Employment Agreement is binding on all employers for every worker of the class, type or group to which it is stated to apply. The Court registers voluntary **Joint Industrial Councils** — negotiating forums within particular industries.

The State also provides Rights Commissioners to assist in resolving disputes, mainly involving individuals.

The **Employment Appeals Tribunal** is composed of employer and worker nominees with an independent chairperson and vice-chairperson. The Tribunal hears disputes over entitlements under legislation including dismissal, notice, redundancy payments, payment of wages and maternity entitlements.

Finance and Currency

The **Central Bank of Ireland**, established in 1942, is primarily responsible for the implementation of monetary policy. As the licensing and supervisory authority for credit institutions it supervises the activities of the commercial banks, acts as a banker to them, ensures compliance with European Monetary System (EMS) obligations and operates an exchange for the clearance of cheques. The

87. The Central Bank of Ireland.

Bank manages the Government's accounts and stock and holds and manages the official external reserves. It publishes an Annual Report, Quarterly Bulletins and Statistical Supplements. From time to time the Bank intervenes in the foreign exchange market to ensure smooth and orderly trading.

Draft legislation published in September 1994 designated the Central Bank as supervisor of stock exchanges in the country — futures and options exchanges are regulated under separate legislation. The Irish Stock Exchange will separate from the London Exchange after the passing of legislation. Irish companies quoted on both the Irish and British Official Lists at the time of separation will be able to have a primary listing on both exchanges.

The **Irish Futures and Options Exchange** (IFOX) opened in 1989. IFOX, a screen-based Exchange with twenty-four members, trades three futures contracts — a long gilt contract, a short gilt contract and a Dublin interbank interest rate contract — and a swap contract.

FINEX Europe, a branch of the financial instruments exchange, which is a division of the New York Cotton Exchange, began trading in Dublin in 1994 at the Dublin exchange facility located at the International Financial Services Centre. FINEX carries on trading on an open outcry basis between 8 am and 1 pm Irish time. When trading ceases in Dublin it switches to New York.

Ireland is a participant in the **EMS** which came into operation on 13 March 1979. The aim of the EMS is to establish a zone of monetary stability in Europe through a system of stable, but adjustable, exchange rates. After the widening of the bands of fluctuation in August 1993, the aim of Irish exchange rate policy continues to be the maintenance of price stability.

The main clearing banks are **Bank of Ireland**, **Allied Irish Banks**, **National Irish Bank** and **Ulster Bank Limited** and these provide a broad range of banking services. Their total assets vis-à-vis residents

*Facing page:
89. The
International
Financial Services
Centre, Dublin.*

*88. The Irish Futures
and Options
Exchange (IFOX).*

amounted to IR£17,757.3m on 31 December, 1993. Other licensed banks are classified into two principal categories: merchant and commercial banks, and industrial banks. The main clearing banks and a large number of the other banks are involved in international banking, including foreign exchange dealing, Euro-currency activities and the Eurobond market.

Merchant and commercial banks are wholesale banks in the sense that the deposits they attract and the loans they make tend to be substantial in magnitude. In addition to general commercial banking services, they manage portfolios on behalf of large investors, such as pension funds, and advise their clients on such matters as mergers and takeovers. This category includes branch affiliates of major European, North American and other international banks as well as domestic banks. Industrial banks are primarily engaged in the extension of instalment credit and similar types of lending under hire-purchase agreements or by way of personal loans. Instalment credit is also provided by hire-purchase finance companies, trading firms and State-sponsored financial institutions.

Building Societies, of which there are five, are also large providers of mortgage credit and other financial services. They are the main providers of mortgage credit in the State and their total assets on 31 December 1993 vis-à-vis residents amounted to IR£7,603.8m.

Apart from the institutions mentioned above there are three State banks. These are **ICC Bank plc, ACC Bank plc** and **TSB Bank.** ICC is a specialist corporate bank concentrating on the small and medium enterprise sector. ACC Bank is a full-scale retail bank providing a range of facilities to personal, corporate, and agricultural customers. TSB Bank is a retail bank concentrating on the personal sector. On 31 December 1993, the total assets of the State banks vis-à-vis residents amounted to IR£3,286.2m.

A number of venture capital institutions make funds available for the development of new ventures which have an identified high growth potential. These institutions usually take a minority equity stake in companies.

Financial Services
The Government's commitment to the development of the financial services sector is evidenced by the establishment of an **International Financial Services Centre** at Dublin's Custom House Dock area. Provision was made in the Finance Act, 1987, for a 10% rate of Corporation Tax on profits on certain trading operations in the Centre. In order to qualify for this rate of taxation, these operations must relate to persons not ordinarily resident in the State and be in foreign currencies.

Under terms agreed with the European Commission, this 10% tax regime is guaranteed until 31 December 2005.

In addition, the Government introduced in the Finance Act, 1989, a revised taxation regime for unit trusts and similar collective investment funds. Such funds are not, in certain circumstances, subject to taxation in Ireland on their income or capital gains.

Trading at the Centre can take the form of global money-management, currency dealing, dealing in foreign currency activities, bonds and equities, insurance and

90. Irish coins.

91. The IR£20 and IR£10 notes depict Daniel O'Connell and James Joyce.

related activities, etc. Operations ancillary to these types of trading may also take place at the Centre provided the Minister for Finance is satisfied that such ancillary operations will contribute to the development of the Centre.

■ *Currency*

The monetary unit is the Irish Pound (IR£ or £) with notes issued in the following denominations: IR£5, IR£10, IR£20, IR£50 and IR£100. There are 100 pence (p) in a Pound. 1p, 2p, 5p, 10p, 20p, 50p and IR£1 coins are issued.

The main attractions of Ireland for visitors lie in its scenery, people, and way of life. The country abounds in rich unspoiled scenery and fresh, unpolluted waters, offering variety and excitement to both the passive viewer and the more active holidaymaker. There are excellent facilities for golfing, walking, riding, cycling, fishing and shooting together with a wide range of other leisure activities.

There is plenty to see and do for those interested in the country's colourful and distinctive cultural heritage. Ireland's history is told in stone — in the megalithic remains, the early Christian churches, the Norman castles, the stately 18th century homes throughout the countryside — as well as the more formal museums, art galleries, theatres and folk parks.

While the tourist industry has its roots in the early 19th century, it was only 30 to 40 years ago that it began to emerge as a major element in the economy. The significance of tourism for the economy has accelerated in the period since 1988, when the Government (supported by the European Union) pledged major additional investment, while setting the industry a five-year objective of achieving substantial increases in revenue and employment.

Foreign exchange earnings, at IR£1,367 million, were 40% higher in real terms in

Tourism

1993 than five years earlier, and 29,000 additional jobs have been created. Directly or indirectly, 91,000 jobs in the economy now depend on tourism. In the same five-year period the domestic foundations of the industry were strengthened by the fact that the number of people taking holidays at home increased significantly, while revenue from the same source increased correspondingly to IR£642 million.

Figure 5.16

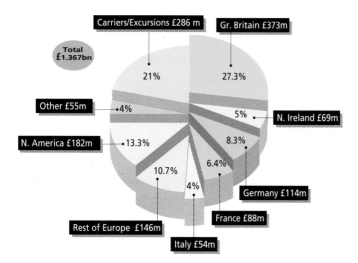

Total £1.367bn

Carriers/Excursions £286 m — 21%

Gr. Britain £373m — 27.3%

N. Ireland £69m — 5%

Germany £114m — 8.3%

France £88m — 6.4%

Italy £54m — 4%

Rest of Europe £146m — 10.7%

N. America £182m — 13.3%

Other £55m — 4%

Foreign Exchange Earnings from Tourism, 1993

Tourism is now the country's fourth largest source of foreign earnings and is the State's highest-earning internationally traded service. It is especially important to the economy of areas which, for geographical reasons, are relatively unsuited to agriculture or industrial development. In this context tourism supports Government policy to achieve balanced economic growth throughout the country.

3.6 million overseas visitors came to Ireland in 1994. The most significant increase in business in recent years has been from Continental Europe — the 1994 total of 990,000 visitors was more than twice that achieved in 1988.

Despite these advances, tourism is still an industry with considerable potential for further development. Accordingly, the Government has embarked upon a new **Operational Programme for Tourism 1994–1999**. This involves the investment of an unprecedented IR£652 million, funded by the Irish public and private sectors and by the European Union. The programme's priorities are to achieve continued improvement in the quality and range of existing products, to enhance standards and service through training, to extend the length of the tourist season and, to this end, to allocate increased resources for marketing.

Major projects planned include a National Conference Centre in Dublin. There will also be substantial investment in improving special interest activities. The fundamental themes of Ireland as a land of unspoilt scenery, wholesome environment and friendly people will underlie a greatly increased marketing campaign for these and other holiday choices.

The programme provides aid to encourage expansion on the part of those already involved in tourism and to attract many more entrepreneurs — home and overseas — into the industry. Targets set for the period up to 1999 are foreign exchange earnings of IR£2,250 million per annum in 1993 real terms, and the creation of an

92. Innisfree island, Lough Gill, Co. Sligo — the inspiration for W.B. Yeats's poem 'The Lake Isle of Innisfree'.

additional 35,000 full-time jobs.

Bord Fáilte Éireann, the Irish Tourist Board, is the State body responsible for the marketing of the industry abroad. Bord Fáilte has offices in major cities in Europe, North America, and in Japan, Australia, and New Zealand.

Seven **Regional Tourism Organisations**, one of which is operated by **Shannon Development** provide a network of information offices and a room reservation service within the State. The Regional Tourist Organisations work with local interests and with Bord Fáilte in the development of resources, and are a vital link between the national body and local communities.

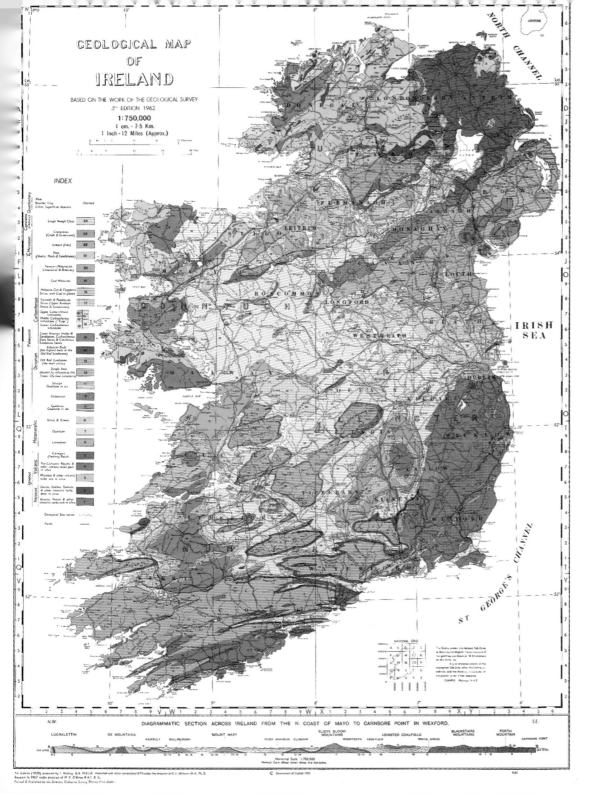

Preceding page:
93. Geological Map
of Ireland.

This page:
94. The University of
Limerick.

Education and Training

Education is compulsory for children aged 6 to 15 years. In 1993/94 there were approximately 960,000 persons in full-time education, more than a quarter of the population of the State. The education system is administered centrally by the **Department of Education** which provides the bulk of current and capital funding. In 1994, £1,982m, the equivalent of 5.6% of GDP, was budgeted for the Department's activities. Education at first and second level schools is free and with effect from the 1996/1997 academic year free education will be introduced at third level also.

First-level Schools

The vast majority of children receive their primary education in **National Schools**, i.e. state-aided primary schools. Each school is run by its own Board of Management, comprising representatives of parents, teachers and local clergy, but receives most of its funding, including teachers' salaries, from the State. There were over 3,317 National Schools in 1993/94 with a total enrolment of 505,800 pupils and a staff of 20,800 full-time teachers. A team of inspectors and advisers ensures that standards are maintained. The present curriculum includes Mathematics, English, Irish, French, History, Geography, Art, Music, Crafts, Social and Environmental Studies and Physical Education. A small number of first-level schools are privately run and do not receive State aid. In 1993/94 first-level schools accounted for approximately 53% of all those in full-time education.

Second-level Schools

Second-level schools cater for students from twelve years of age upwards. There are various types of second-level schools. **Secondary schools** are privately owned, many by religious communities, but most of their expenditure is funded by the State.

95. National School children.

There were 461 Secondary Schools in 1993/94 with a total enrolment of 224,035 pupils and a staff of 12,514 full-time teachers paid by the State. There are two courses of study. The **junior cycle** is a three-year course leading to the award of the **Junior Certificate**. The **senior cycle** is a two-year course leading to the award of the **Leaving Certificate**, the basic qualification for admission to third-level education. There is an optional **transition year** available at an increasing number of schools during which students may pursue non-examination subjects. The curriculum for both cycles covers a wide range of subjects including Mathematics, English, Irish, Modern Languages, History, Geography, Science subjects and Physical Education.

Comprehensive and **Community schools** are State-owned second level schools. There were 73 Comprehensive and Community schools in 1993/94 with a total full-time enrolment of 48,850 pupils and a staff of 2,715 full-time teachers.

Vocational schools are owned and operated by the State through local Vocational Education Committees. Vocational schools were, originally, mainly concerned with technical education. In general, however, the range of subjects now offered is similar to that offered in other second level schools. There were 248 Vocational Schools in 1993/94 with a total full-time enrolment of 94,760 pupils and a staff of 5,120 full-time teachers.

Second-level teachers must have a university degree and a postgraduate diploma in education. Teachers of technical subjects must have the appropriate qualifications in their areas of competence. Approximately 38% of all full-time students were in second-level education in 1993/94. Approximately 50% of students who complete the Leaving Certificate course proceed to third level education.

Third-Level Education

There are four universities in the State. **Dublin University** comprises one college, **Trinity College.** The **National University of Ireland (NUI)** has colleges in Dublin, Cork, Galway and Maynooth. The **University of Limerick** and **Dublin City University** were established as independent universities in 1989.

The **Regional Technical Colleges** and the **Dublin Institute of Technology** place a heavy emphasis on applied science and on technological education, particularly in the area of the new technologies. Other third-level educational establishments cater for medicine, law, art, music and teacher training.

Centres for microelectronics research are located at **University College Cork** and at the **Plassey Technological Park** in Limerick. Other third-level institutions specialise in particular areas. Barristers and solicitors are trained in Dublin at the **Honorable Society of King's Inns** and at the **Incorporated Law Society of Ireland,** respectively. The **Royal College of Surgeons in Ireland** provides medical qualifications independently of the university medical schools. There are also a number of colleges of music and art.

96. Dublin Institute of Technology.

The total number of students attending full-time third-level courses in 1993/94 was approximately 86,300. This compares with 62,800 students attending full-time courses in 1988/89.

Training
FÁS, the Training and Employment Authority, is responsible for the operation of training and employment programmes, the provision of an employment/recruitment service, an advisory service for industry, and support for co-operative and community based enterprise. Priority is given to those persons facing greatest difficulties in the labour market, including the long term unemployed and early school leavers.

CERT is the national organisation for the education, recruitment and training of personnel for the tourism, hotel and catering industries. It is responsible for training at hotel and catering schools.

Teagasc — the Agriculture & Food Development Authority, provides agricultural advisers to assist farmers. It operates a number of agricultural colleges and grant-aids other, privately-owned, colleges. Its priorities include the education and training of young farmers.

Science and Technology

Historical Background
Ireland has been represented in science and technology by such distinguished names as **Robert Boyle**, the 17th century physicist, **John Tyndall** (1820–93), who lent his name to a wide variety of scientific and technological discoveries, and **Lord Kelvin** (1824–1907), who is renowned for his work on transatlantic cables. While these worked in international circles, others such as **William Rowan Hamilton** (1805–65), the inventor of quaternion calculus, **William Parsons** (1800–67), builder of the world's first great telescope, and **Nicholas Callan** (1799–1864), the father of battery technology and magnetism, maintained a strong tradition at home. **Ernest T. Walton** of Trinity College, Dublin, won the Nobel Prize for Physics in 1951.

Irish institutions have also been innovators. The Dublin Society (later the **Royal Dublin Society**), established in 1731, was among the first schools of science and became a model for other such societies. The establishment of the **Royal Irish Academy** in 1785 gave Irish science and technology an independent focus. The work of these bodies, together with the universities, made Dublin an important centre for mathematics and astronomy in the 19th century.

Science and Technology Today
The Government recognises that science and technology are central to economic and social development. It is a cornerstone of policy to ensure an adequate flow of well-educated graduates, diploma holders and people with third level educational certificates in science and related disciplines.

Total Government allocation to science and technology amounted to IR£498 million in 1993. The education and training of scientists, engineers and technicians in formal courses was the main area of expenditure followed by technical services in the health sector. A major expenditure in the manufacturing industry area was under the **Science and Technology for Industrial Development Programme** of the Department of Enterprise and Employment.

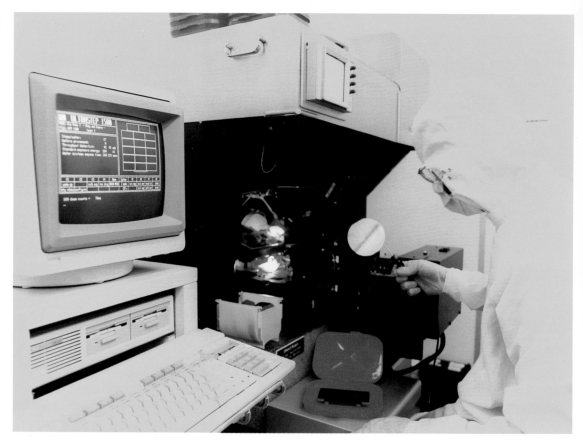

97. The National Microelectronics Research Centre, Cork.

The Department's **Office of Science and Technology**, has responsibility for co-ordinating Ireland's input on science and technology issues at the level of the European Union and other international fora.

State research institutes play a major role in providing advice and consultancy in support of economic and social development. These include **Teagasc**, which provides advisory research, education and training services for agriculture and the food industry, **Forbairt**, which is responsible for the development of indigenous industry and for providing investment support for science and technology in industry, third level education

colleges, and other specialised centres, and **Forfás**, the policy and advisory board for industrial development.

Other State research institutes include the **Health Research Board**, involved in research in health, health services, and epidemiology, and the **Environmental Protection Agency**, which provides environmental and related services to support the environmental infrastructure programmes of the Department of the Environment and the local authorities.

The Schools of Theoretical Physics and of Cosmic Physics of the **Dublin Institute for Advanced Studies** pursue fundamental research and train advanced students in original research methods.

■ *Research and Development*
Total expenditure on research and development was estimated at IR£376 million in 1993 or 1.2% of GDP. Expenditure in the business sector accounted for 65% of the total.

■ *Research and the Higher Education Sector*
Expenditure on research in the colleges of higher education was estimated at IR£79 million in 1993. A new feature of university sector research is the programmes in advanced technologies. The overall goal of the programmes is to enhance the performance of industry through research and technology transfer activities. Programmes have been established in advanced manufacturing technology, biotechnology, materials, optoelectronics, power electronics, software and telecommunications.

Ireland is a member of the **EUREKA**

programme of technological research which is intended to enable Europe to exploit technology for world competitiveness, and of the **European Space Agency**. Ireland is party to a number of bilateral co-operation agreements in science and technology, predominantly with European countries, to facilitate collaboration between research bodies and individual researchers.

The health system is primarily funded from general taxation and is publicly provided although private health care retains a considerable role. Public health expenditure in 1994 amounted to IR£2,085 million or 5.9% of GDP. Private health expenditure was estimated at a further IR£660 million or approximately 2% of GDP. The **Department of Health** also has responsibility for services such as social work, adoption, child care etc.

The Health Strategy *Shaping a Healthier Future,* published in 1994, aims to enhance the health and quality of life of the population. In future, it is intended to assess the health care system by its effectiveness;

Health and Social Security

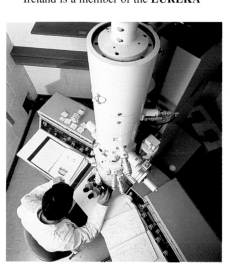

98. Research at the National Technological Park, Plassey.

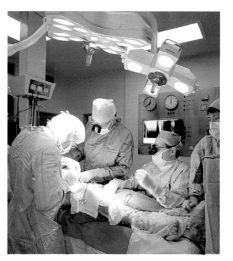

99. Public-service healthcare.

i.e. the benefits received by the users of services, rather than by levels of service. A high degree of emphasis is placed on preventative medicine. In particular, efforts are being made to address the main contributors to premature mortality such as smoking, alcohol abuse, poor nutrition, lack of exercise, etc.

Main Causes of Premature Death

Life expectancy is 72.2 years for men and 77.7 years for women. Premature deaths arise mainly from what are often referred to today as "diseases of civilisation". These included cardiovascular disease (heart attacks and strokes) and cancer. At 361 deaths per 100,000 of population in 1991 the rate of death from cardiovascular disease is higher than the average in the European Union. The rate of death from stroke has fallen to the EU average in recent years but the rate of death from heart attacks, while falling also, is still above average. The death rate from cancer is 245 per 100,000 and is increasing. This is above the EU average. There has been a marked drop in deaths from accidents. At 49 deaths per 100,000 the rate is considerably below the EU average.

Administrative Structure of the Services

At national level, the Department of Health sets the budget for the health services, plans the overall development of the services and initiates regulatory and legislative change. The provision of health care at regional level is the responsibility of the eight **Health Boards**. **Voluntary hospitals and agencies**, although outside the health board structure, are an important and integral part of the health care system. Voluntary hospitals,

mainly run by religious orders, report to the Department and receive their funding from it.

Eligibility for the Public Health Services

Everybody ordinarily resident in Ireland has either full or limited eligibility for the public health services; the type of eligibility is determined by a means test. Approximately one-third of the population has full eligibility and these have free access to the complete range of services. The remainder of the population have limited eligibility; this entitles them to consultant and hospital care subject to small charges. They obtain GP services and prescribed drugs privately. They can avail of refund schemes in cases of excessive expenditure on prescribed drug expenditure.

Private Health Insurance

Approximately one-third of the population opts to take out private health insurance. Prior to 1994 a State company, the **Voluntary Health Insurance Board**, had a virtual monopoly on the provision of such insurance. While this monopoly has now been abolished, any insurance company operating in the country is required to do so on a community rating basis, whereby everybody in a scheme pays the same premium regardless of risk.

The Delivery of Services

The health services can be divided into three main categories:

— **Community-based services**, including the general practitioner service, home nursing, preventative and detection programmes such as school health examinations and immunisation programmes, and dental, ophthalmic, aural and other services.

— **General Hospital Services**. These include 63 acute public hospitals which are owned and funded by the Health Boards; voluntary hospitals which are operated by their own boards which are funded by the Department of Health; and 24 private hospitals, which operate independently of the Department. The public hospitals have approximately 12,000 beds; the average length of stay is 6.5 to 7 days.

— **Special Hospital Services,** which provide treatment for the mentally ill.

Social Security

The Social Welfare system seeks to be comprehensive in its coverage of social need, responsive to new and changing needs, and fair, consistent, simple and cost effective in administration.

The services provided by the **Department of Social Welfare** can be categorised as follows:

• **social insurance benefits** based on pay-related social insurance (PRSI) contributions. These contributions are compulsory for employees and the self-employed;

• **social assistance allowances** payable to people who do not have insurance cover. These payments are made on the basis of the claimant satisfying a means test;

• **universal services** such as child benefit and free travel for the elderly, which do not depend on PRSI or means.

The **social insurance scheme** provides cash benefits for people who become ill, unemployed, take maternity leave or reach pensionable age (66 years). The scheme allows for payments for orphans, people who become widowed, and women deserted by their husbands. A range of dental and optical services is available to insured workers and their dependent spouses.

The **social assistance scheme** includes payments for people who are unemployed, blind, orphaned, people who reach pensionable age and for lone parents. There are special schemes for working families on low incomes and a supplementary scheme to help people in difficult financial circumstances.

A number of schemes are designed to enable the long term unemployed to improve their chances of gaining employment. Grant schemes exist to support voluntary and community activity. These include support for locally based women's groups, the Community Development Programme, etc.

Figure 6.1

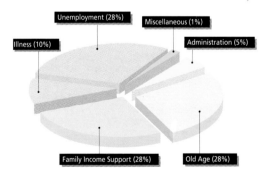

Unemployment (28%)
Miscellaneous (1%)
Illness (10%)
Administration (5%)
Family Income Support (28%)
Old Age (28%)

Expenditure on Social Welfare by Programme

At the end of 1994 some 820,000 persons were in receipt of a weekly social welfare payment. Expenditure on Social Welfare amounted to IR£3,776m, equal to 10.7% of GDP, in that year.

Communications

The postal and telecommunications services are operated by State companies, **An Post** (the Post Office) and **Bord Telecom Éireann**.

■ Postal Service

A limited mail service between Dublin and London was in existence as early as 1561. However, the initial development of the service began in 1638 when post-stages were organised between Dublin and other major towns. In 1711 a unified post office was created covering Ireland and Britain. The introduction of the penny post in 1840 greatly increased the volume of mail. Responsibility for postal services was taken over by the Department of Posts and Telegraphs in 1922, which administered the system until the establishment of An Post in 1984.

An Post, a state-owned company, operates the national postal service and has an extensive network of post offices. It directly employs almost 8,000 people, with 3,000 more involved in sub-offices. The company's turnover in 1993 was almost IR£272 million, from which it made a profit before taxation of over IR£7 million. Over one million items of mail are handled each day. They are delivered from Monday to Friday to households and businesses throughout the country, with a rate of over 94 per cent next-day delivery of first-class mail. On the retail side, over IR£3 billion worth of transactions are carried out each year at almost 2,000 post offices throughout the country. These transactions include the payment of pensions and other welfare benefits, bill payment services, licence sales, savings services etc.

Special facilities for business users include **Postaim**, offering reduced rates for bulk posting of addressed advertising material and **Publicity Post**, for the delivery of unaddressed advertising matter.

Other services include **SDS-Special Distribution Services** — a dedicated business unit through which **An Post** now

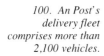

100. An Post's delivery fleet comprises more than 2,100 vehicles.

101. Telecom Éireann.

provides all its services for parcel and urgent document distribution. **Post GEM** is the company's electronic communications subsidiary. **An Post** also provides banking and foreign exchange facilities at most company offices.

■ *Telecommunications*

Telecom Éireann, established in 1984 as a commercial State enterprise, provides telecommunications services to 1.17 million subscribers.

The telecommunications network is one of the most digitalised in the world, offering national and international voice, mobile, data, value added and integrated services. IR£2.5 billion has been invested in the system over the past 15 years. A further IR£750 million will be invested over the next 5 years to maintain and improve the technological sophistication of the infrastructure and to expand services.

With a turnover of IR£871 million in 1993/4, and profits of IR£81 million, Telecom Éireann is ranked among Ireland's "Top 10" companies.

Transport

■ *The Road Network*

Ireland's network of public roads extends for 92,300km. The network comprises national roads (5,400km), regional roads (10,600km) and local roads (76,300km). There are 26 km of road per 1,000 population; roughly twice as much as in Belgium, France or Denmark, and over three times as much as in the Netherlands, Italy or Spain.

Within the network, **national primary roads** (2,700km) are the major long distance through-routes linking the principal ports, airports, cities and large towns. **National secondary roads** (2,700km) are the medium distance through-routes connecting important towns. The national route system represents 6% of the overall road network but carries 38% of total road traffic. **Regional roads** are the main feeder routes into, and provide the main links between, the national roads. The remainder of the network (80%) is made up of **local roads** which serve the transport needs and requirements of urban areas and local communities.

102. Tivoli over-pass, Cork city.

The **National Roads Authority** was established in 1993 to oversee the development of the roads network. It has overall responsibility for planning and supervising the construction, improvement and maintenance of the network. It has a mandate to complete the development of the primary network by the year 2005 with a view to enabling inter-urban travel to take place at a speed of 80 kilometres per hour.

The **Operational Programme for Transport** maps out a strategy for a total investment programme of IR£1.65 billion in roads infrastructure over the six years 1994–1999.

Road Transport

The importance of road transport to the economic and social development of the country is illustrated by the following:

- inland transport depends predominantly on roads. These carry 96% of passenger and 90% of freight traffic;

- vehicle numbers quadrupled between 1960 and 1994 and are expected to continue to increase into the early years of the next century;

- the number of goods vehicles over 8 tons unladen weight also quadrupled between 1960 and 1994 and is expected to continue to increase;

- the total number of licensed vehicles on the roads at the beginning of 1995 was 1,202,273; this was the highest number ever recorded.

Most road freight business is handled by around 3,000 private licensed hauliers with a combined fleet of over 10,000 trucks. Many manufacturing and processing enterprises also operate their own truck fleets.

CIE (Coras Iompair Éireann — Irish Transport System), is the statutory body providing public transport services. CIE has two subsidiary bus companies: Bus Átha Cliath/Dublin Bus and Bus Éireann/Irish Bus, which operate services in the capital and throughout the country, respectively. Through its subsidiary, Íarnród Éireann/Irish Rail, CIE is responsible for the operation of rail services.

Bus Átha Cliath has a fleet of nearly 850 buses and provides an extensive service over a 1,000 sq km area of the Dublin conurbation. It caters for a population of more than a million and over 160 million passenger journeys are made with the company each year.

Bus Éireann provides public transport by coach outside the Dublin area. The company's services include a network of inter-urban bus services, rural bus services throughout the country, and urban bus services in Cork, Limerick, Galway and Waterford. There are over 60 million passenger journeys on Bus Éireann services each year.

CIE International Tours specialises in coach tours of Ireland. The company has offices in London, New York, Paris, Dusseldorf and Dublin. Apart from CIE, 1,400 private bus owners operate a fleet of 3,600 buses. Most of these operators concentrate on non-scheduled services such as school transport and coach tours.

103. DART.

104. Bus Átha Cliath's 'City Swift'.

105. Íarnród Éireann operates ten 201 class locomotives.

Rail Transport

The present railway network consists of a radial system of 1,900 route kilometres with Dublin as the focal point. The rail gauge is 1,600 mm, differing from the rest of Europe but common to the Republic and Northern Ireland. CIE's rail company **Iarnród Éireann**/Irish Rail operates passenger and freight services. Rail (including DART) carries 26 million passengers annually, providing direct intercity services between Dublin and Cork, Limerick, Galway and other significant centres of population. Railfreight carries 633,000 tonne kms and 85% is import/export traffic. Iarnród Eireann also operates a roadfreight service.

The cross-border Cork/Dublin/Belfast line, a high speed Trans European Network, is being upgraded with 75% co-financing by the EU.

The **Dublin Area Rapid Transit (DART)** provides a passenger service over 38 km of track using electric motive power along the Dublin coastal area. The system includes the original stretch between central Dublin and Dun Laoghaire, the world's first commuter railway, opened in 1834.

Aviation

The international airports at Dublin, Shannon and Cork handle about 8 million passengers and 94,000 tonnes of freight annually. The busiest airport is Dublin with annual traffic of 6 million passengers and over 65,000 tonnes of freight. Many international airlines provide scheduled services between Ireland and destinations in Europe and North America. There is also a large volume of charter traffic.

Irish airlines providing scheduled and/or charter services to and from Ireland include **Aer Lingus**, **CityJet**, **Ryanair** and **Translift Airways**. A number of small aviation companies provide passenger, freight and helicopter services within the country using the network of regional airports. These are located at Donegal, Galway, Kerry, Knock, Sligo and Waterford.

Aer Lingus is the State owned-airline. It operates a fleet of 29 aircraft comprising mainly B737's and Airbus A330's. The airline also operates Fokker 50's and Saab 340B's. Scheduled services are operated to 27 cities in the United Kingdom, Europe and North America. Charter services are operated to a wide range of destinations. The airline carries approximately 4 million passengers and 45,000 tonnes of freight annually.

Dublin, Shannon and Cork international airports are managed by **Aer Rianta**, a public company. Aer Rianta's subsidiary, **Aer Rianta International**, manages a number of airports abroad and operates duty-free facilities at several locations throughout the world.

Shipping

External trade is exceptionally dependent on seaports which account for 76% of trade in volume terms and 60% of exports in value terms. Techniques in shipping and cargo handling have changed dramatically in recent years and ports have developed their facilities accordingly. Dublin and Cork are the State's multi-modal ports, handling all types of unitised and bulk cargoes. The construction of a new load-on/load-off (Lo/Lo) terminal at Belview has enabled Waterford Harbour to become potentially the largest and most up-to-date Lo/Lo handling port in the country.

106. Stena Sealink's 80,000 h.p. Stena HSS, the world's biggest high speed ferry.

Rosslare, Dun Laoghaire, Cork and Dublin are the country's passenger/car ferry ports. Other harbours deal predominantly in bulk cargoes. The largest of these are located at Limerick, Foynes, Drogheda, Dundalk, Galway, Wicklow, Arklow and New Ross.

A number of companies provide passenger car-ferry services to and from Ireland. **Irish Ferries** operate daily services to Britain on the *Dublin-Holyhead* and *Rosslare-Pembroke* routes. **Irish Ferries** are preparing to introduce a new Superferry on the *Dublin-Holyhead* route from 1995.

Stena Sealink has daily services to and from Britain on the *Dun Laoghaire-Holyhead* and *Rosslare-Fishguard* routes. The company intends introducing a new high speed service vessel from 1995 on the *Dun Laoghaire-Holyhead* route. This ferry could be capable of crossing the Irish Sea in 99 minutes.

Irish Ferries operate services to France, connecting *Rosslare* and *Cork* with *Le Havre* and *Cherbourg* and a further service, to *Roscoff*, is planned for later in 1995. **Brittany Ferries** run weekly services from *Cork* to *Roscoff* between March and October, and from May to September they link *Cork* with *St. Malo*. **Swansea Cork Ferries** run a daily service from *Cork* to *Swansea* between March and January.

The Irish registered shipping fleet (100 gross tons and over) comprised 79 ships totalling 161,786 gross tons at 30 June, 1994.

■ *Newspapers and Periodicals*

Newspapers have been published in Ireland for over three centuries. The very first periodical news-sheet, entitled *An Account of the Chief Occurrences of Ireland*, was published in February 1659. Later, in the closing years of the 17th and the early part of the 18th centuries, there was a flood of more solidly established newspapers, such as *Faulkner's Dublin Journal*, which was founded in 1725 and lasted for a century, and *Saunders's News-Letter* (1755–1879). Of the newspapers founded in this period only the *Belfast News Letter* has survived. First published in 1734, the *News Letter* is the country's oldest newspaper.

The 19th century produced many successful newspapers, among them the *Dublin Evening Mail* (1821–1962) and the *Freeman's Journal* (founded in 1763) which in 1924 was absorbed into the *Irish Independent*, one of the present national daily newspapers. Many daily and weekly newspapers were published in the main towns and cities. Among the titles published in Cork which had a population of 85,745 in 1851, were the *Free Press*, the *Herald* and the *Constitution*. In the same year Galway, with a population of 23,695, had six newspapers; Tralee, County Kerry, with a population of 15,156 had eight (five weekly and three evening papers) and Waterford, with a population of 11,257, published two evening papers.

The country's first penny newspaper was *The Irish Times* which was launched by

Media

107. Current newspaper mast-heads.

THE IRISH TIMES
Irish Independent
The Cork Examiner
IRISH Press THE STAR

owned enterprises, independent of the larger publishing groups.

A wide variety of magazines and periodicals is also published.

Circulation Figures ABC January–June 1994	
Irish Independent	144,023
Irish Times	93,066
The Star*	70,980
Cork Examiner	52,041
Irish Press	38,806
Evening Herald	93,648
Evening Press	55,532
Evening Echo	25,710
Sunday World	270,066
Sunday Independent	253,291
Sunday Press	158,924
Sunday Tribune	81,503
Sunday Business Post	29,710

* Not including Northern Ireland sales

Major Lawrence Knox in 1859. The *Irish Independent* was founded in January 1905. Éamon de Valera, then leader of the *Fianna Fáil* party and later Taoiseach and President, founded *The Irish Press* in 1931 and its success led to the launching of *The Sunday Press* (1949) and the *Evening Press* (1954).Seven morning daily newspapers are published. Four are based in Dublin: the *Irish Independent*, *The Irish Press*, *The Irish Times* and *The Star*; two are published in Belfast: the *News Letter* and *The Irish News* and one, *The Cork Examiner,* is published in Cork. Four evening newspapers are published: the *Evening Press* and *Evening Herald* (Dublin), the *Belfast Telegraph*, and the *Evening Echo* (Cork). Five Sunday newspapers are produced in Dublin: the *Sunday Independent*, *The Sunday Press*, *The Sunday World*, *The Sunday Tribune* and *The Sunday Business Post*; *The Sunday Life* is published in Belfast.

There are over 90 provincial newspapers, usually published weekly. The largest-selling provincial newspaper is the *Kerryman*. Many of the provincial newspapers are family-

■ Radio and Television

Radio Telefís Éireann (**RTÉ**) is the national broadcasting service. Radio broadcasting commenced on 1 January, 1926 and the television service was inaugurated on 31 December, 1961. RTÉ is a statutory corporation. The RTÉ Authority consists of nine members, appointed by the Government. Under the Authority, the chief executive is the Director-General. There are separate programme divisions for Radio, Television and News, with management, technical and support systems in engineering, television production facilities and information technology.

As the principal broadcaster in the country, RTÉ fulfils a public service remit by providing a comprehensive range of programming. The service has a nationwide communications network with an increasing emphasis on regional input and news gathering.

Radio services are broadcast nationwide on VHF in stereo on three networks. **Radio 1** (over 9,500 hours broadcast each year), **2FM** and **Raidió na Gaeltachta** in both Irish and English, provide news, current affairs, music, drama and variety, features, and programmes on agriculture, education, religion and sport. **Radio 2FM** is a 24-hour music and chat channel with a high proportion of popular current affairs. **Raidió na Gaeltachta** is the dedicated Irish language radio medium. In addition, **FM3** offers classical music and **Cork Local Radio** reflects regional activity in Munster. RTÉ Radio services can be received via the **Astra satellite system** throughout Europe and, in part, on the **Galaxy 5** satellite to North America. The latter service is also available worldwide to computer users on the World Wide Web at *http://town.hall.org/radio/wrn.html*

RTÉ Television broadcasts nationwide on

108. 'Biddy' (played by Mary McEvoy) and 'Miley' (played by Michael Lally) in the long-running RTÉ drama 'Glenroe'.

RTÉ 1 and **Network 2**. These operate as complementary channels, with an aggregate output of approximately 10,000 hours each year. Over half of output is home-produced with an increasing proportion being commissioned from independent producers. A further one hour per day is to be supplied to the projected Irish language television channel, **Teilifís na Gaeilge**, which is expected to commence broadcasting in 1996. Informational programming on television is especially popular with viewers, and there is an increasing commitment to using television drama to promote the best new and established talent in writing, acting and directing.

Atlantic 252 is a commercial long wave radio station which can be received throughout the country and Britain, and in parts of Europe.

RTÉ, jointly with Telecom Éireann, owns and operates **Cablelink** Ltd., one of Europe's largest cable television companies. In addition to RTÉ services, Cablelink provides four British television channels, and twelve satellite channels, and is currently poised to provide **MMDS** (Microwave Multipoint Distribution System) services to smaller towns and rural areas. **Aertel**, a teletext information service, is currently received free of charge by 40% of homes.

RTÉ's staff of approximately 1,900 includes writers, journalists, musicians, actors, singers, producers, artists, and designers. The service is the largest provider of music of all kinds in the country, employing over 150 full-time musicians, and engaging many more on a freelance basis.

The service's finances are derived from licence fees (40% of income in 1993),

An Account of the chief
OCCURRENCES
OF *IRELAND*;
Together with some Particulars from
ENGLAND:

From Wednesday the 15 *of Febr. to Wednesday* 22 *of February.*

February the 15. 1659.

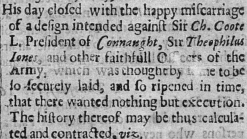

His day closed with the happy miscarriage of a design intended against Sir *Ch. Coote* L. President of *Connaught*, Sir *Theophilus Iones*, and other faithfull Officers of the Army, which was thought by some to be so securely laid, and so ripened in time, that there wanted nothing but execution. The history thereof may be thus calculated and contracted, *viz.*

The Army having by their Declaration on the 14 of *December* last, declared against the sinfull interruptions put on the Parliament, thought it their duty thoroughly to pursue the ends of that Engagement; and finding the interruption given the Parliament in 1648, to be owned and justified by those now sitting, thought themselves bound in duty to declare for the secluded Members : for prevention whereof, some fanatick spirits prevailed with Sir *Hardress Waller* to remove the Convention of Officers appointed at the Custom-house (their usual place of their Meeting) to the Castle, which they knew being better fortified with Guns than Reasons, was the more likely to give success to their intended Design of surprising the said Sir

A   *Charls*

109. *"An Account of the Chief Occurrences of Ireland" – Ireland's first periodical news-sheet, published in Dublin in February, 1659.*

110. 'Questions and Answers', a weekly current affairs programme on RTE.

advertising sales revenue (55% of income in 1993), and ancillary income. In 1993 total income was almost IR£131.6m with expenditure of almost IR£124m. **RTÉ Commercial Enterprises** incorporates the **RTÉ Guide**, the country's largest selling weekly magazine, with a circulation of 180,000.

■ *Independent Broadcasting*
Independent local and national radio services are arranged through The **Independent Radio and Television Commission**. The Commission, a Government appointed body, is also to arrange for the provision of an independent television service. The local

independent commercial radio sector now consists of twenty-one franchise stations around the country, including two stations in the Dublin area. Two non-profit making stations — one community station and one special interest (Irish language) station — have been licensed in the Dublin area, and there are plans to introduce further community stations in selected areas throughout the country.

Literature in Irish

■ *The Early Period*

Ireland's Golden Age of Christianity and learning began in the sixth century of our era and lasted until the ninth. A large corpus of writing is extant in the language of the period, OLD IRISH. The corpus consists of lyrical and devotional poetry, prose sagas, homilies, historical and legal material, and scholarly commentaries on biblical and Latin grammatical texts.

This significant literature, the earliest extensive record in any European vernacular north of the Alps, was written by scholars who were educated in the monastic schools of the period. While they composed poetry which was obviously personal, the extent to which other parts of the extant corpus were their own creation or a record of orally transmitted tradition is a question on which modern scholars are not fully agreed. Much of the saga literature, for example the epic *Táin Bó Cúailnge* (The Cattle-Drive of Cúailnge), purports to represent a pre-Christian society, but monastic writers supplied the narrative structure, and many details of the content may equally be the product of their imaginations. So also it has been demonstrated that even the earliest law texts show ecclesiastical influence. The conclusion that they also preserve elements of an ancient pre-Christian tradition seems irrefutable, but the exact relationship between tradition and innovation in the earliest literary record remains to be determined.

Irish literature of this early period was not without influence on later European literature. The theme of tragic love, as found in the legend of Tristan and Isolde, is thought to derive ultimately from Irish sources, such as the tales of Deirdre and Naoise, Líadan and Cuirithir, and Gráinne and Diarmaid. And tales of fantastic voyages, such as *Imram Maíle Dúin* (The Voyage of Máel Dúin) and the Latin *Navigatio Brendani* (The voyage of Brendan), captured the imagination of medieval Europe.

113. A scribe from Giraldus Cambrensis' Topographia Hiberniae.

114. Monastic settlement at Skellig Michael, Co. Kerry.

The Middle Irish Period

The period of the Viking incursions and settlements, when political strife was endemic, is frequently regarded as a period of literary stagnation. This is the MIDDLE IRISH period. Certainly, it lacks the freshness and vitality of the Old Irish period, but it produced all the same a substantial body of literature. This includes the long sequence of 150 cantos on biblical themes called *Saltair na Rann* (The Versified Psalter), a work believed to have been composed in AD 988 by Airbertach Mac Cosse Dobráin, though this is disputed by some scholars; the historical poems of Flann Mainistrech (c. AD 1000–56); the extensive compilations in verse and prose of legends about famous places, known as *Dinnshenchas* ('lore about prominent places'); adaptations to the form of Irish prose sagas of Latin epics such as Virgil's *Aeneid* and Lucan's *Bellum Civile*. To the end of the period belongs the powerful satire on monks and literary men, *Aislinge Meic Con Glinne* (The Dream of Mac Con Glinne).

The Early Modern Period

Following the social and political changes brought about by the arrival of the Anglo-Normans in 1169, there begins what is called the EARLY MODERN or CLASSICAL MODERN period in Irish language and literature. It lasted until the seventeenth century and is characterized by a more modern standard literary language. This standard was cultivated principally by the secular literary schools which were maintained by professional poets or literary scholars called *filidh* in Irish, or in English often called 'bards'. Verse compositions by these professional poets form a substantial part of the literature which is extant from the period. Much of the professional poets' verse consists of eulogies to their aristocratic patrons, but there is also a substantial body of extant religious and personal poetry. Among the more eminent professional poets of the Early Modern period were: Donnchadh Mór Ó Dálaigh (1175–1244); Muireadhach Albanach Ó Dálaigh (1180–1250); Gofraidh Fionn Ó Dálaigh (1320–87), who was regarded by members of the profession who came after him as the greatest exponent of their craft; Tadhg Óg Ó Huiginn (+1448); Tadhg Dall Ó Huiginn (1550–91); Eochaidh Ó hEodhusa (1567–1617); and one of the last in the tradition, Fear Flatha Ó Gnímh (1602–40). As even this much abbreviated list reveals, the profession was largely hereditary.

Fenian, or *Ossianic*, literature flowered in the Early Modern period. This genre was composed around the legendary *Fionn Mac Cumhaill* and his warrior band, or *fian(n)*; *Oisín*, anglicized *Ossian*, was Fionn's son. The earliest reference to Fionn is in a text which belongs to the eighth or ninth century, but the first extended treatment of Fenian/Ossianic themes in extant literature is in *Agallamh na Seanórach* 'the old men's discourse', which belongs to the second half of the twelfth century. The *Agallamh* is a large compilation of prose tales combined with narrative and lyrical verse, and unified by the device of supposing that the pagan Oisín, or a fellow-warrior Caoilte, survived to meet St. Patrick, accompany him on his mission around Ireland and, in each place which they visited, recount to him the various adventures which Fionn and his warriors had experienced there. Thus, like many other compositions in the traditional literature, the *Agallamh* reflects the persistent influence of the *Dinnshenchas*.

Fenian/Ossianic themes continued until the eighteenth century to inspire verse and prose compositions. In 1750, a Co. Clare poet, Mícheál Coimín, composed his *Laoi Oisín ar Thír na nÓg* 'Oisín's song about the Land of Youth', and after 1760 the genre became internationally known through the purported translations of James MacPherson (1736–96). His work was loosely based on the Scottish Gaelic oral tradition, with which as a native of the Highlands he was well acquainted.

In the Early Modern period much narrative and pious matter was adapted from external sources, mainly from French and English, and love poetry in the *amour courtois* genre was very successfully practised by professional poets and by members of the aristocracy. Among the noblemen whose compositions survive are: the third Earl of Desmond, Gearóid Mac Gearailt (+1398); Lord of Tyrconnell, Maghnus Ó Domhnaill (+1563); and Sir Piaras Feirtéir of Corkaguiny (+1653).

■ *The Post Classical Period*
The Early Modern period came rapidly to an end following the overthrow of the Gaelic order in the seventeenth century. The transition is marked in prose by compilations intended to conserve the record of Gaelic civilization, such as the great synthesis *Annála Ríoghachta Éireann* 'annals of the kingdom of Ireland' written in 1632–36 under the supervision of Mícheál Ó Cléirigh (1575–1645), or Séathrún Céitinn's narrative history *Foras Feasa ar Éirinn* 'foundation of knowledge about Ireland', completed around 1634. Séathrún Céitinn (1570–1645) was deprecated as an amateur by professional historians of the native tradition, but he was a master of prose and his work remained extremely popular until recent times.

As for verse, the transition was marked by an abrupt decline in patronage for poets and by the replacement of the classical syllable-count metres by stress-count metres called *amhrán*. The *amhrán* metres make their appearance fully fledged, in various elaborate patterns and frequently in conjunction with an arcane style. They can hardly, therefore, represent the development of a more simple medium to suit a less sophisticated audience, as has sometimes been suggested, and their provenance is still a matter of controversy. The most prominent poets of the period were Séathrún Céitinn, Pádraigín Haicéad (1600–54), a Dominican priest who was much involved in the politics of his day, and Dáibhí Ó Bruadair (1625–98), who strove in vain to maintain the traditional status of the professional poet and wrote bitterly about the transformation of Irish society. Aogán Ó Rathaille (1670–1728), regarded as one of the greatest poets in the Irish canon, was one of the last to receive some patronage for his work, but it scarcely amounted to more than charity. Indeed his unfortunate benefactors, whatever their attitude to his compositions may have been, were hardly in a position to provide him with the estates and fees which the professional poets of the Early Modern period would have received without question.

The Eighteenth and Nineteenth Centuries

Even after aristocratic literary patronage had totally ceased in the eighteenth century, Irish literature continued to be cultivated by members of the clergy, farmers, artisans, and schoolmasters. Such people diligently maintained the manuscript tradition and composed topical and personal verse, sermons and pious matter, and some prose narrative. They included Seán Ó Neachtain (1655–1728) and his son Tadhg (c.1680–c.1750); Eoghan Ó Caoimh (1656–1726); Seán Ó Murchadha (1700–62); and, perhaps most prolific of all, Mícheál Óg Ó Longáin (1766–1837). Industrious scribes and sober hard–working people, who devoted what energy they could in adverse times to the preservation and cultivation of literature in Irish, they were overshadowed in the popular imagination by the more rakish and often more talented personalities who for many typify the period. Among the latter were: Peadar Ó Doirnín (1704–68); Aindrias Mac Craith (1708–95); Donnchadh Rua Mac Con Mara (1715–1810); Eoghan Rua Ó Súilleabháin (1748–84); and pre-eminently the mathematics master Brian Merriman (1747–1805) who wrote the long poem *Cúirt an Mheán Oíche* 'the midnight court', which has attracted more numerous and illustrious translators than almost any other composition in Irish.

Merriman and Raftery (Antoine Ó Reachtabhra 1784–1835), or indeed others of earlier date, have often been described as the last representatives of the tradition. By 'tradition' here is presumably meant the concept of literature and the themes and styles of versification which had characterized composition in the Irish language, at least since the end of the Early Modern period. The reality is not quite so clear-cut. Though the nineteenth century was a period of severe disruption and decline for the Irish-speaking community, the cultivation of Irish literature was not abruptly abandoned. Mícheál Óg Ó Longáin, for instance, was active until his death in 1837.

(283)

Air ḋaċ an ofṇ do bị aṛoiċ
maṛ ṛeulċ aịṛ aṇoịg do bị
'ṛa ṛaoṛṇịg da ḃṛaịċṛea aoṇeaċ
do ḃeaṛċa do ṛeaṛċ don mnaoị.
Dṛṇṛoeaṛ ḟịonn ag ịaṇṛaịd ṛgeṛt
aịṛ mnaoị ṛeịṃh na ċċṛaċ nóịṇ
Dṛịaṛṇaịd mo ṇịg don ġṇṛịg ṇgịl
an ḃṛacaịd. ċṛ mo ċhoịṇ ṛa ċoịṇ?
Aṇṇ do ṛeịlg nị ċhṛịl mo ṛpeịṛ.
Ịṛ nị ċhaca mé do ḃa choịṇ
a ṇ̇ị na ṛeịṇe ġaṇ ċaịṇ
Ịṛ meaṛa ḷom ṛaċ mo ġṛịl
Aṇ é do ċ̇ịle do ṛuaịṇ ḃaṛ
a ịṇġ̇ean ċlaịṛ̇, ṇo do mac
ṇo caṇ é an ṛaċ ṛa ḃṛịl do ċṛ̇ị
aịṇṛoịṇ ċṛ̇ịṇ Ịṛ ṛịlṇe oṛeaċh
Ṇo caṇ aṛ aḃṛịl do ḃṛón
a aịṇṇịṛ ṛg na mboṛ mịṇ
ṇo an ṛeṛoịṇ ċṛuṛċaċċ (d ṛịonn)
Ịṛ ṛuḃaċh ḷom do ḃeịċ maṛ ċhịm
ḟaịl ofṇ do bị ṛo mo ġlaịc
do ṛaịṛ̇ ịṇġean ṛg na ḃṛoịċ ṛeịṇ
ċṛ̇ịṇ̇ịṇ dom laịṛ ṛan ċṛṇeaḃ
ag ṛịṇ maḃḃaṛ da ḃeịċ ịṃ̇ḃeịṇ
ġeaṛa naṇ ċhṛlaịṇg ṛaoċ
cṛịṇịṃ do ċ̇onn a ṛg na ḃṛhịaṇ
maṛ ċṛugaịṇ mṛḃaịṇṇe ċṛugam ċaịṇ aịṇ
ċṛ̇ịċ ṛe ḃeaṛ na ṛṛeaḃ ṇoịaṇ
Ṇịoṇ ċhṛulaịṇg ḟịonn ċṛṇ na ṇġeaṛ
ċṛ̇aċ ċ̇ṛịṇ ḃe aṛaịṛ̇ ṛo na ċ̇neṛ̇ ġléịṇ
ċṛuaịṛ̇ ġo ḃṛuaċ an loċa ṛ̇aṃ
ḋ ċhuṛaịṛleaṃ mna na mbaṛṛ ṇéịṛ̇.

O o 2   Ꝺo

Besides him, the following at least deserve mention: Seán Ó Coileáin (1754–1817), a somewhat pedantic poet whose best-known poem is *Machnamh an Duine Dhoilíosaigh* 'the melancholy man's reflections'; Dáibhí de Barra (1757/8–1851), a prolific writer and scribe; Pádraig Phiarais Cúndún (1777–1857), who, having emigrated with his family to the United States in 1826, continued to write and correspond in Irish and apparently never learned English; Amhlaoibh Ó Súilleabháin (1780–1837), whose diary for the years 1827–35 is the earliest surviving example of the genre in Irish literature; Tomás Rua Ó Súilleabháin (1785–1848), in his verse a vigorous supporter of Daniel O'Connell; Art Mac Bionaid (1793–1879), a stonemason who in his day enjoyed a high reputation as a scribe and literary scholar; Aodh Mac Dónaill (1802–67), who in addition to verse wrote a treatise on natural history; Nioclás Ó Cearnaigh (1829–74), an industrious writer and collector who, however, left some confusion in his wake by ascribing to earlier authors many of his own compositions. Even in the twentieth century, poets such as Mícheál Ó Gaoithín (1904–74) of West Kerry can only be regarded as representatives of an unbroken poetic tradition.

Raftery, in fact, did not belong so much to this strand of the Irish literary tradition as to that of folk-poetry, which was no doubt vigorously cultivated at all periods. However, folk-poets of the late eighteenth and nineteenth centuries flourished late enough to ensure that their compositions came to the attention of the folklorists and collectors of the Irish revival. Raftery (1784-1835) owes his renown to Douglas Hyde's edition, *Songs ascribed to Raftery*, which appeared in 1903. Other equally commendable exponents of the folk-verse tradition were: Diarmaid Ó Súilleabháin (1760–1847); Máire Bhuí Ní Laoghaire (1770–1830); Seán Ó Duinnlé (+1897); Mícheál Ruiséal (+1928). To this category of primarily oral literature must also be assigned *Caoineadh Airt Uí Laoghaire*, the powerful lament by Eibhlín Dubh Ní Chonaill (1748–1800) for her husband Art Ó Laoghaire, who was murdered in 1773. This outstanding example of an oral funerary lament, or *caoineadh*, survived long enough in the folk tradition to have been written down by nineteenth-century collectors. How accurately it has been preserved one cannot now ascertain.

116. Writers in Irish.

Pádraic Ó Conaire

Máirtín Ó Cadhain

Seán Ó Ríordáin

Máire Mhac an tSaoi

Michael Hartnett

Breandán Ó hEithir

Liam Ó Muirthile

Seán Ó Tuama

Nuala Ní Dhomhnaill

Máirtín Ó Direáin

■ *The Irish Revival and Aftermath*
As the revival gathered momentum and a wider readership was cultivated, a new generation of writers in Irish began to look to contemporary European models. Peadar Ó Laoghaire (1839–1920), while not the most imaginative of writers, was a major influence in the development of a new literary diction. In a comparable style, Pádraic Ó Conaire (1882–1928) and Patrick Pearse (1879–1916) introduced the modern short story which became a very popular genre in Modern Irish. Among its more effective practitioners are: Liam O'Flaherty (1897–1984) who also wrote in English; Seosamh Mac Grianna (1901–90); Máirtín Ó Cadhain (1907–70); Donncha Ó Céileachair (1918–60); Seán Mac Mathúna (b.1936); and Pádraic Breathnach (b.1942).

The modern novel has not been as thoroughly cultivated. Peadar Ó Laoghaire wrote a folk–novel, *Séadna*, and a historical novel, *Niamh*, the former being more successful than the latter. Séamas Ó Grianna (1891–1969), under the pen-name *Máire*, wrote romantic novels which gained a wide popularity. Other estimable novelists are: Seosamh Mac Grianna; Máirtin Ó Cadhain, author of *Cré na Cille* 'the earth of the graveyard'; Pádraig Ua Maoileoin (b.1913); Eoghan Ó Tuairisc (1919–82); Dónall Mac Amhlaigh (1926–89); Breandán Ó hEithir (1930–90); Diarmaid Ó Súilleabháin (1932–85); Pádraig Standún (b.1944); Alan Titley (b.1947); Pádraig Ó Cíobháin (b.1951); Ciarán Ó Coigligh (b.1952); and Séamus Mac Annaidh (b.1964).

Drama has also had its exponents: Douglas Hyde (1860–1949); Mícheál Mac Liammóir(1899–1978); Máiréad Ní Ghráda (1899–1971); Séamas Ó Néill (1910–1981); Eoghan Ó Tuairisc; Brendan Behan (1923–64); Seán Ó Tuama (b.1926); Críostóir Ó Floinn (b.1927).

The Irish revival movement, through its concern to conserve the vernacular Irish tradition, led to an appreciation of the copious oral literature which in Irish survived well into the twentieth century. As a result, an exceptionally fine collection of material has been recorded and is in the keeping of the Department of Irish Folklore at University College Dublin. A proportion of the material has been edited and published. In addition, some of the best traditional story-tellers were persuaded to record their own experiences, and from this developed a distinct genre of Gaeltacht autobiography. Two examples of the latter have become internationally known classics: *An tOileánach* 'the islandman' by Tomás Ó Criomhthain (1856–1937), and *Fiche blian ag fás* 'twenty years a-growing' by Muiris Ó Súilleabháin (1904–50).

Modern poetry, which began with Patrick Pearse and his contemporaries, reached full maturity in mid-century in the works of Máirtín Ó Direáin (1910–88), Seán Ó Ríordáin (1917–77), and Máire Mhac an tSaoi (b.1922). Foremost among its present-day exponents are: Pearse Hutchinson (b.1927), Deirdre Brennan (b.1934), Tomás Mac Síomóin (b.1938), Michael Hartnett (b.1941), Mícheál Ó Siadhail (b.1947), Biddy Jenkinson (b.1949), Gabriel Rosenstock (b.1949), Dáithí Ó hÓgáin (b. 1949), Liam Ó Muirthile (b.1950), Michael Davitt (b.1950), Nuala Ní Dhomhnaill (b.1952), Áine Ní Ghlinn (b.1955), Cathal Ó

Searcaigh (b.1956) and Colm Breathnach (b.1961).

While poetry is the genre most frequently translated into English, in reality it may also be the genre most resistant to assimilation into an English-language literary tradition. Although a majority of the population can now read such work only in translation, the writing of Irish-language poets remains central to a definition of the country's contemporary literary tradition. Speakers, readers, and writers of Irish are marginal in number only. They are, more crucially, the living and vibrant expression of a literary culture which spans more than fourteen centuries, and they are the warranty for the continuing linguistic and cultural diversity of the island of Ireland.

Literature and Drama in English

Irish writing in the English language is called Anglo-Irish Literature to distinguish it from classical English literature on the one side and literature in the Irish Language on the other. The sense of tension in the word Anglo-Irish reflects a question of national identity which has energised that literary tradition from William Molineux's *Case of Ireland Stated* (1698) to the Report of the New Ireland Forum of 1983, from Swift's *Gulliver's Travels* (1726) to Flann O'Brien's *At Swim Two Birds* (1939). Jonathan Swift (1667–1745) was a contemporary of Aogán Ó Rathaille, last of Gaelic Ireland's dynastic poets. Though the two lived on the same island their worlds hardly touched, and there is irony in the fact that one tradition was born while the other expired. Ó Rathaille's theme was the decay of the old Gaelic Catholic order; Swift's theme was the humiliation of the Irish

Protestant nation at the hands of the London parliament. Neither writer heard the other's voice. Yet the development of an Irish

literary tradition was to involve the mutual discovery and interpenetration of these two nations, their languages, aspirations and culture.

The first great development in the 18th century, colonial, period was almost totally Protestant, its temper classical, its perspectives cosmopolitan, its focus London with its clubs, theatres and town houses. It

117. Edmund Burke (left) with his friend, the radical Whig politician Charles James Fox (Thomas Hickey, 1741–1824).

could be said that the English comedy of manners from the Restoration to the rise of Romanticism was the creation of brilliant Irishmen, George Farquhar, William Congreve, Charles Macklin, Oliver Goldsmith and Richard Brinsley Sheridan. The only sign of 'Irishness' in these writers was their affection for that comic personage — bibulous, irascible, generous, eloquent and sentimental — who came to be known as the 'stage Irishman'.

These writers were typically educated at Protestant grammar schools and Trinity College Dublin. They gravitated to London, centre of the literary universe, and quickly became absorbed into that imperial consciousness. Swift, Steele, Burke and Sheridan were active in British politics. When Burke wrote about the miseries of Ireland it was in terms of a global responsibility that took in the French Revolution and the revolt of the American colonies. It was the duty of Augustan literature 'with extensive view to Survey Mankind, from China to Peru', and that perspective is reflected in the essays of Steele and the fiction and poetry of Goldsmith — though some critics have seen the withering of an Irish peasant community in his *Deserted Village* (1770).

With Swift it was different. His appointment as Dean of St Patrick's, Dublin, in 1714 at once marked the end of his hopes for high ecclesiastical office and the start of his passionate involvement in politics. The problem of Anglo-Irish identity has seldom been better expressed than in his *Drapier's Letters*, where he attacked Westminster for imposing its will on the Dublin parliament: 'Am I a Free-man in England, and do I

become a slave in six hours by crossing the Channel?.' The feeling of resentment against England was a theme for pamphlet, satire and ballad through the century until the granting of legislative independence to the Irish parliament in 1782.

The new 'Patriot Parliament' brought not only a flowering of political thought and oratory — Grattan, Flood and Curran being the exemplary figures — but a surge of scholarly and poetic interest in that Gaelic Ireland that had seemed to be dying on its feet in the figure of Aogán O Rathaille at the beginning of the century. Charlotte Brooke's *Reliques of Irish Poetry* (see page 142) made available authentic Ossianic poems which had been only glimpsed in the famous forgeries of James MacPherson a generation previously. Edward Bunting published his *Ancient Music of Ireland* in 1796 and Thomas Moore was setting words to these airs in his famous *Irish Melodies* before the turn of the century. The spirit of the French Revolution and of the Romantic Movement in literature fuelled the patriotic balladry of the rebellion in 1798. But the sense of optimism and creativity which characterised these last years of the century was crushed by the Act of Union (1800) which abolished the Irish parliament and reduced the level of cultural activity.

The decades that followed were dominated by the 'regional novel'. Its pioneer was Maria Edgeworth, daughter of a Protestant landlord, whose powerful influence on his own regional fiction of the Scottish Highlands was acknowledged by Sir Walter Scott. In her novels, most notably *Castle Rackrent* (1800) and *The Absentee* (1812) she addressed the vexed problem of

Anglo-Irish identity, especially the role of the landlord divided between the lure of London and the responsibilities of his stewardship. Apart from their literary intentions these novels were directed at an English readership in an attempt to explain the condition of Ireland. Her lead was followed by Lady Morgan, and by the Catholic novelists, Gerald Griffin, John and Michael Banim and the prolific William Carleton, born to Irish-speaking parents in Tyrone in 1794. His *Traits and Stories of the Irish Peasantry* provides the most authentic and vivid account of life among Ireland's rural poor anywhere available.

Throughout the first half of the 19th century there was steady work in Gaelic manuscript study, folklore and translation by scholars like John O'Donovan, Eugene O'Curry and Sir Charles Petrie, and such poets as Jeremiah Joseph Callanan, Edward Walsh, Samuel Ferguson and James Clarence Mangan. Their activities centred largely on the *Ordnance Survey* of the 1830s, the *Dublin University Magazine* and later *The Nation* newspaper; this had been founded in 1842 to renew the cause of Irish nationalism which had in a sense been shelved during O'Connell's campaigns for Catholic Emancipation and later for Repeal of the Union. The *Nation*, addressing itself to an indigenous readership and insisting on the concept of autonomous Irish nationhood, could be said to have heralded the end of 'regionalist' writing. The cultural dimensions of nationality had by now been adumbrated in a substantial body of poetry based on native sources, historical, social and mythological. Therefore, when William Butler Yeats found himself at the head of a literary renaissance

in the last years of the century he claimed the *Nation* poets as his cultural ancestors:

Know, that I would accounted be
True brother of a company
That sang to sweeten Ireland's wrong
Ballad and story, rann and song

Nor may I less be counted one
With Davis, Mangan, Ferguson.

The two most arresting events of the literary renaissance were, arguably, the performance of Yeats's *Countess Cathleen* and Edward Martyn's *The Heather Field* on a double bill in Dublin in 1899, and the publication of George Moore's *The Untilled Field* (1903). Both events involve the interpenetration of the two cultures, both have resonances well beyond Ireland, and both contain in embryo the essential features of the movement. Yeats's play, performed by an English company of actors, explored a traditional theme; Martyn's brought Ibsen's social realism to bear on Irish rural life. Moore, on the other hand, had returned to Ireland having made himself a reputation for adapting Zola's naturalism to the English novel in *Esther Waters*. He was approached by the Gaelic League — recently founded by Douglas Hyde with the aim of reviving Irish as a spoken language — to write a number of simple stories which might be translated into Irish to act as models for its fledgling writers. As he proceeded with the task he realised that he could do for his own country what his friend, Turgenev — an exiled landlord like himself in Paris — had done for Russia in his *Sportsman's Sketchbook*.

Moore remained in Ireland for the first decade of the century, long enough to write his finest novel, *The Lake*, and to compose his imaginative history of the literary revival, *Ave, Salve, Vale*, which began to appear in 1911.

Meanwhile, the theatre movement prospered. It found a permanent home in the Abbey Theatre in 1904, and by then a body of distinguished playwrights had emerged under its auspices — John M. Synge, Lady Gregory, Pádraic Colum and Yeats himself. Synge was the greatest and most controversial: his *Playboy of the Western World* caused a famous riot on its production in 1907. His death in 1909 ended the first great phase in the Abbey Theatre's history.

a strenuous involvement with social and political issues. His contemporary, George Russell ('AE'), continued in that vein of Celtic mysticism which he had shared with the early Yeats, though his 'first disciple', James Stephens, revealed a more adventurous and experimental spirit. In 1912 Stephens published, side by side with his most mystical volume of poems, *The Hill of Vision*, his novel of the Dublin slums, *The Charwoman's Daughter* and his classic fantasy, *The Crock of Gold*. His experiments with prose fiction showed the way to a succession of fantasists including Flann O'Brien, Mervyn Wall, Eimar O'Duffy, even

118. The Well of the Saints (J.M. Synge) at the Abbey Theatre.

In poetry Yeats moved from that early mode of the 'Celtic Twilight' which had reached its climax in *The Wind Among the Reeds* (1899) to the engaged, muscular and combative poetry of *The Green Helmet* and *Responsibilities* (1914), whose title betokens

James Joyce himself, as in the Celtic grotesqueries of the Cyclops episode of *Ulysses*.

Joyce chose the expatriate route towards his chosen territory, what his hero Stephen Dedalus had called 'silence, exile and cunning'. The route had already been taken by Boucicault whose witty melodramas like *The Colleen Bawn* and *The Shaughraun* relied to a great extent on the stock figure of 'the stage Irishman'; and by Oscar Wilde and George Bernard Shaw who had dominated the London stage in the 1890s. After his dazzling success with *The Importance of Being Earnest* and *The Portrait of Dorian Gray*, Wilde died tragically in the last year of the century. Shaw continued to entertain London with his plays, prefaces and conversation for another fifty years.

Joyce's devious and precarious course took him to Trieste, Pola, Rome, Paris and Zurich while he created a body of prose fiction that was to transform the novel. *A Portrait of the Artist as a Young Man* dramatised the inner consciousness of the growing artist with a suppleness and intensity of style never matched before or since in the *bildungsroman*. *Ulysses* (1922) deployed the mythic outline of Homer's *Odyssey* to make its hero, a Dublin Jew named Leopold Bloom, the universal modern citizen and Dublin the archetypal metropolis of western civilisation. Joyce's relentless experiments with language and form went on to make *Finnegans Wake* at once the most brilliant and impenetrable prose narrative in the history of literature.

The short story continued to be a favourite vehicle for Irish writing. Daniel Corkery's first collection, *A Munster Twilight* (1916), affectionately explored the ethos of his native province. His *Hounds of Banba* celebrated the guerilla warfare of the War of Independence in which his fellow Corkmen, Frank O'Connor and Seán O Faoláin, were actively involved. Their first volumes,

Oscar Wilde

Jonathan Swift

Patrick Kavanagh

Seán O'Casey

Louis MacNiece

Brendan Behan

Seamus Heaney

J.M. Synge

119. *Irish Writers.*

O'Connor's *Guests of the Nation* and O Faoláin's *Midsummer Night's Madness* in the early 1930's, cast a colder eye on the armed struggle and on the quality of life in the new State. Beside them loomed the novelist and short story writer Liam O'Flaherty, whose vision of elemental life on the Aran Islands brought a new lyricism to the form. Mary Lavin's *Tales from Bective Bridge* (1942), with its passionate contemplation of life in the midlands, revived a sense of organic form which looked back to Joyce and forward to James Plunkett's evocations of Dublin in his collection, *The Trusting and the Maimed* (1959).

The tradition of the 'Protestant Nation' which Edith Somerville and Martin Ross had inherited from Edgeworth, Charles Lever and Charles Lover and developed in their witty *Irish R.M.* series, found its next great exponent in Elizabeth Bowen (1900–1973). Bowen's novels, *A World of Love* and *The Last September*, explore the life style of the Cork gentry in a changing social and political world. The line continued through the light satiric fiction of Christine Longford and W. J. White to the brilliant short novels of Jennifer Johnston and the fiction of William Trevor, both of whom reflect the contemporary tragedy of Northern Ireland.

The second great phase of the Irish theatre began with Seán O'Casey's 'three blazing masterpieces', *The Shadow of a Gunman, The Plough and the Stars* and *Juno and the Paycock* in the 1920's. In the same decade Denis Johnston effectively introduced the techniques of Expressionism in *The Old Lady Says No*. Other notable dramatists of the time were Lennox Robinson, T. C. Murray, Paul Vincent Farrell and, a little later, Walter Macken and M. J. Molloy.

The contemporary theatre also displays both talent and vitality. Brian Friel, who had already achieved an international reputation with *Philadelphia, Here I Come* (1964), reached new heights of excellence with *Translations*, *The Faith Healer* and *Making History* (1988). Thomas Murphy, who had an early success with *Whistle in the Dark* (1961), scored a hit with his brilliantly experimental *Gigii Concert* (1983). His *Bailegangaire* (1985) was given its premiere by Druid Theatre Co. with Siobhán McKenna. This was followed by *Too Late for Logic* in 1989. Hugh Leonard, one of the few to conquer London and New York at the same time, has crowned his achievement with two brilliant sister plays, *Da* and *A Life* (*Da* has now been filmed). Other notable contemporary playwrights are Frank McGuinness with *Observe the Sons of Ulster Marching Towards The Somme* (1985) and *Innocence* (1986); Michael Harding with *Strawboys* (1987) and *Una Pooka* (1989); Dermot Bolger with *The Lament for Arthur Cleary* (1989) and *Blinded by the Light* (1990).

The most daring of experimental dramatists has been Tom MacIntyre whose theatrical rendering of Kavanagh's *Great Hunger* on the one hand, and of the inner workings of Swift's creative psyche in *The Bearded Lady* on the other, have called forth the Abbey's full resources of dance, mime, music, feature, costume and decor. The works of Thomas Kilroy (*Talbot's Box*),

120. Commemorative stamps featuring Nobel Prizewinners for Literature (from left): Samuel Beckett, George Bernard Shaw and W.B. Yeats.

J. B. Keane (*The Field*), Graham Reid (*The Death of Humpty Dumpty*) and Bernard Farrell (*I do not Like Thee Doctor Fell*) continue to sustain the liveliest period of Irish theatre since the death of Synge.

After the death of Yeats the world of poetry was divided between Austin Clarke and Patrick Kavanagh. Austin Clarke (1896–1974) moved into his great period in 1938 with a volume of lyrics, *Night and Morning*. His poetry was especially notable for its range of prosodic resource and the intensity with which it rendered what he called 'the drama of racial conscience'. Kavanagh (1904–1967) is considered by many to have written the greatest long poem of contemporary Ireland in *The Great Hunger* with its tragic hero, a small farmer in Monaghan.

A number of outstanding poets began to publish in the 1960's — Thomas Kinsella, John Montague, Derek Mahon, Richard Murphy, Anthony Cronin, Michael Longley, Eavan Boland, Brendan Kennelly, and Seamus Heaney. Kinsella's *Nightwalker* (1968) and Montague's *The Rough Field* (1972) addressed in very different idioms painful questions of personal and national identity. The former's *Butcher's Dozen* was a controversial public response to the Widgery inquiry, while Montague's long masterpiece remains a pertinent reflection on the tangled inheritance of Northern Ireland. Mahon, Longley and especially Heaney have evolved sophisticated responses to the matter of Northern Ireland with each in his own way facing the equally bleak questions of identity posed by the common human inheritance of a terrible century. Seamus Heaney (b. 1939) is Ireland's best known poet of the present day, noted for his lyric evocation of the Ulster countryside with its tragic underdeposit of history. He has been Oxford Professor of Poetry and presently teaches at

121. Books published in Ireland.

Harvard. Among his works are *Station Island* (1984) and *Seeing Things* (1991). Brendan Kennelly and Paul Durcan have garnered huge followings for poems that, in their different ways, offer a radical critique of modern Irish life. Michael Hartnett stands out as a poet whose unillusioned lyrics reclaim for the English language tradition characteristic themes of the part-submerged high-Gaelic tradition. All of these poets work in the central, lyric, tradition which comes down to us unbroken from the Gaelic, mediated through Yeats in the English language. Eavan Boland, a lyric poet with a keen sense of history and its exclusions, gives these inheritances a new cast, examining her life as a woman and Irishwoman of the late twentieth century from a considered feminist perspective. Her work has been influential in empowering a new generation of women poets.

The towering figure in fiction as well as drama after the death of Joyce was the Nobel Prize winner, Samuel Beckett (1906–1989). Beckett's first novel, *Murphy* (1938), launched him on an exploration, at once bleak and hilarious, of humanity's absurdity *sub specie aeternitatis*, reaching its climax with the great trilogy, *Molloy, Malone Dies, The Unnamable*. Other versions of the absurd were pursued by his contemporary, Flann O'Brien (1911–1966) in *At Swim – Two-Birds* and *The Third Policeman*. Benedict Kiely and Brian Moore both began their writing careers in the fifties and have since kept in step in the range and variety of their themes and their experiment with fictional form. In the sixties *The Barracks* and *The Dark* marked the appearance of John McGahern as a remarkable novelist. Of the older generation, Aidan Higgins and Edna O'Brien have constructed memorable Irelands in their different ways, but the rising generation of prose writers, most notably Dermot Healy, Evelyn Conlon, Anne Enright, Colm Toibin, and Glenn Patterson, are all striking out into individual territories, apparently uninfluenced by their older contemporaries.

The seventies saw Francis Stuart's crowning achievement in the novel, *Black List, Section H*, a psychological self-portrait of great intensity. It was also in this decade that John Banville published the first of his subtle, reflexive fictions, *Long Lankin*. He has since completed his trilogy, *Doctor Copernicus, Kepler* and *The Newton Letter*, in which he dramatises the birth of modernism in human consciousness. His novel *The Book of Evidence* was short-listed for the Booker Prize in 1989.

Ireland in the 1990's is celebrating a second literary renaissance. With the writers of the 1960's still for the most part vital and publishing, there is now a new generation of considerable talent coming through: in prose Hugo Hamilton, Dermot Healy, Patrick McCabe and Roddy Doyle — winner of the 1993 Booker Prize for his novel *Paddy Clarke Ha Ha Ha* — have appeared to considerable critical acclaim as have, in poetry, Ciaran Carson, Paul Muldoon and Medbh McGuckian from the North, together with Eiléan Ni Chuilleanáin, Paula Meehan, Thomas McCarthy, Philip Casey and Matthew Sweeney from the South. In theatre, Sebastian Barry, Dermot Bolger, Declan Hughes, Billy Roche and Marie Jones are already playwrights of considerable achievement.

Publishing

One of the most healthy developments of recent years has been the emergence of a thriving book publishing industry. Valued at about IR£29 million p.a., approximately 70% is educational publishing and the remainder falls into the general sector. With literature in Irish and English, publishing in Ireland is carried on in both languages.

There was very little publishing in English in the period following the Second World War. One of the pioneers in the field was Dolmen Press, led by Liam Miller, which published the works of poets Thomas Kinsella, Richard Murphy and John Montague in the early 1950's.

The *Irish University Press* had been a large house and when it was wound up in 1984 a great number of trained personnel were released onto the market. The new houses founded in the 1970's and '80's included *Poolbeg, Wolfhound, O'Brien, Blackstaff, Brandon* and *Lilliput*. Dedicated to the publishing of literature in particular, they grew throughout the 1980's. The report: '*Developing Publishing in Ireland: Cothú na Foilsitheoireachta in Eirinn*' in which the eminent British publisher, Charles Pick, surveyed the performance of a number of small Irish houses, was issued in 1988. The report found that there is considerable scope for growth in publishing particularly if export potential is concentrated upon.

Among the houses surveyed were the fast-growing women's publisher, *Attic Press*, the Irish-language house, *Coiscéim*, and *Wolfhound, Brandon* and *O'Brien*. The report was considered by the *Arts Council* which, together with *An Bórd Tráchtála* (the Irish Export Board) and *Forbairt* (the State agency assisting indigenous business), has provided grant-aid to encourage the growth of publishing. A greater involvement in the British and European markets is expected to be a feature of the later 1990s. In regard to the European market, Irish publishers are particularly interested in the promotion of translations.

A new agency has been established to promote literature abroad, both in Irish and in English — the *Ireland Literature Exchange/Idirmhalartám Litríocht Éireann* (ILE). ILE promotes Irish literature and, in particular, literary translations. The Translation Fund of ILE assists foreign publications with the translation fees on works of Irish literature.

Art

The origins of Irish art are obscure, dating back to perhaps as early as 3,000 BC in tombs and sanctuaries along the Boyne Valley. This art was abstract and three-dimensional, expressing itself through spirals, loops and geometric forms on kerbstones and granite slabs, following the contours of stone pillars at passage graves and burial tombs in Newgrange and Knowth. In the pre-Christian era, the dominant form belongs to the La Tène period of Celtic art, which relates to a broader culture spanning the continent of Europe.

Uninterrupted by the Roman incursions which fragmented Celtic culture in Britain, Irish society remained based on small tribal units whose structure was not affected in a radical way by the coming of Christianity in AD 432. Artists and craftworkers continued to enjoy a privileged position in society, producing bronze and enamel work, as well as some manuscript illumination. By the 8th and 9th centuries, technical advances and the

122. The Great Book
of Ireland (Leabhar
Mór na hÉireann);
left: 'Da Tagte Es' by
Samuel Beckett
(1906–1989). First
published in 1934,
this version of the
poem was written by
Beckett just four days
before his death.
Right: Study of
Samuel Beckett by
Louis Le Brocquy.

FOR SAM

LOUIS LE BROCQUY
25 DECEMBER 84

123. Gold Boat; probably 1st Century A.D.

scholarship encouraged by the many monastic settlements throughout the island brought Celtic art to its greatest heights. Illuminated manuscripts such as the Book of Durrow, a copy of the Gospels, combined abstract panels of interlocking forms and spirals with a limited palette of red, green and yellow, turning at times into highly stylised animal shapes. These forms were developed in such works as the Book of Dimma and culminated in the late 8th century in the Book of Kells (see page 20), where the previously central abstract motifs were organised around the figure of Man, whether as Christ, as Devil or as Angel. The artist's palette now included several shades of blue, brown, yellow, green, red and mauve.

A centuries-long period of invasions, civil wars and tyranny began with the Viking incursions from the mid-9th century. One form which in particular survived this period was stone sculpture, from the simple High Cross at Carndonagh to the Cross of Moone which depicts scenes from the Gospels. Metal and other craftwork also flourished: the most notable example is the Cross of Cong, a shrine for a fragment of the True Cross which was made early in the 11th century by order of the high king.

The Norman invasion and later the dissolution of the monasteries under English rule interrupted and finally changed the system of patronage through which Irish art had flourished. Guilds of urban craftworkers now emerged, influenced from England and continental Europe; a new ruling class sought images of itself from painters and sculptors. By the mid-17th century the decorative arts of goldsmithery, plasterwork, silver, glass and furniture flourished under the auspices of guilds such as the Goldsmiths' Company of Dublin. Easel painting replaced tapestry and wall painting and a 'painters' guild', formed in 1670, included in its number such artists as Garrett Morphy (fl. 1680–1716) and James Lathan (1696–1747), who had studied at Antwerp.

The prosperity of the 18th century and the influence of the Enlightenment throughout the fields of philosophy and aesthetics produced an atmosphere in which great public buildings were commissioned. Examples include the Parliament House, now the Bank of Ireland, by Edward Lovett Pearce, and the Custom House and Four Courts by James Gandon. At the same time, men and women of ideas were debating one of the century's most influential works on aesthetics, Edmund Burke's *A Philosophical Enquiry into the Origin of our Ideas of The Sublime and Beautiful,* published in 1756 but probably written earlier. Two major painters of the period, George Barret (1732–84) and James Barry (1741–1806) were protegés of Burke and embody in their work many of his aesthetic ideas. With such ideas as the excitement of pain or danger (the sublime) or love (the beautiful), the subject-matter of painting broadened to include historical and some landscape work, often with classical or mythological allusions. Topography, too, was

a central concern and was best expressed by James Malton, a former draughtsman in Gandon's practice, who drew his *Views of Dublin* between 1790 and 1791.

The Act of Union in 1800 removed the centre of power from Dublin to London. Many artists emigrated to London; others stayed at home and formed structures which were to support the arts for many years to come. The foremost of these was the Royal Hibernian Academy, established in 1823 as an amalgamation of previously splintered artists' groups. The Academy's annual exhibitions established a reliable market for its members, and stimulated debate on the concerns of painting. A major tradition of landscape painting emerged, led by James Arthur O'Connor (1792–1841), amongst whose influences was 17th century Dutch engraving.

George Chinnery (1774–1852), William Sadler (1782–1839) and Gaspare Gabrielli (fl. 1805–30) were also concerned with the art of landscape through watercolour, gouache and oil, as were Cecilia Campbell (1791–1857), Henry O'Neill (1798–1880) and Edward Hayes (1797–1864). Daniel Maclise (1806–70) and William Mulready (1786–1863) had significant impact on English art, as had Francis Danby (1793–1861) whose work was characterised by the Romanticism which influenced much Irish painting at the time. Sculptors such as John Henry Foley (1818–74), John Lawlor (1820–1901) and Samuel Ferris Lynn (1834–76) worked with British sculptors to produce the Albert Memorial. Foley's work includes the memorials to Oliver Goldsmith and Edmund Burke in Trinity College Dublin, and the memorial to Daniel

O'Connell in O'Connell Street, Dublin.

Impressionism began to influence Irish art with the work of Nathaniel Hone, John Butler Yeats, John Lavery, Sarah Purser, Walter Osborne, William Orpen and Roderic O'Conor. Foremost among painters of this period, however, was Jack B. Yeats, (1871–1957), whose appeal continues to the present day. Brother of the poet and playwright William, Jack Yeats's work focussed upon key moments and actions in the lives of individuals. The best-known artist of the period was Paul Henry who had studied at Whistler's studio in Paris before settling in Connemara to paint landscapes based on a palette of matt blues and greys.

The assurance with which Yeats, Orpen and Henry had painted Irish life came less readily to that generation of artists whose lives coincided with the Civil War and the establishment of the Irish Free State. The cultural aspirations of the young State were based on those of a nationalist tradition, historically separate from the ruling class which had been the main patrons of art in colonial times.

Some artists travelled abroad to absorb the heady advances of Cubism, Futurism, Dada. Mainie Jellett and Evie Hone returned from a period of work with André Lhote and Albert Gleizes in Paris to become leaders of the modern movement in Irish painting. Others belonged to a landscape tradition of academic realism: Seán Keating, Maurice MacGonigal, Sean O'Sullivan were foremost in this school.

By the end of the second World War, the modern movement had begun to challenge the academic tradition through such artists as Louis Le Brocquy and Norah McGuinness. They, together with Hone and Jellett, had in 1943 founded the *Irish Exhibition of Living Art* as a *salon refusé* for work which was unacceptable to the annual exhibitions of the Royal Hibernian Academy.

Sculptors like Oisín Kelly and Hilary Heron pioneered the use of new casting techniques and promoted the concept of an Irish vernacular sculpture. The Living Art Exhibition became a forum for artists whose influences were derived from the international language of visual art: Patrick Scott, Gerard Dillon, Gerda Fromel, Nano Reid, Barrie Cooke, Cecil King and Camille Souter, as well as artists like Patrick Collins and Tony O'Malley whose work derived from landscape. Living Art's activity continues to the present day, headed in the sixties and seventies by such artists as Brian King, Michael O'Sullivan, Tim Goulding, Michael Farrell, Martin Gale, Robert Ballagh and by immigrant artists including Alexandra Wejchert, Erik Adriaan van der Grijn, Adrian Hall. In the eighties, Living Art extended its concerns to video and performance art as well as painting and sculpture, exhibiting the works of Aileen MacKeogh, Nigel Rolfe, Eilis O'Connell, Helen Comerford, Joe Butler, Cecily Brennan and a host of emerging artists. A strong new expressionist movement has emerged from the Independent Artists group, represented by Michael Kane, Patrick Hall, Brian Maguire, Patrick Graham, Eithne Jordan, Michael Mulcahy and Michael Cullen. Sculptors of achievement include Michael Bulfin, John Behan, Edward Delaney, Conor Fallon and John Burke.

Facing page: 124. Reclining Nude Before a Mirror, Roderic O'Conor (1909).

125.

126.

127.

125. Bird Table,
(1969),
Norah Mc Guinness.

126. Artist in the
Country, *(1973),*
Nano Reid.

127. Nutt, *(1988),*
Brian King.

128.

130.

130. Undercover,
(1993),
Kathy Prendergast.

129.

131.

8. Ark of
eaming, *(1991),*
ddy Graham.

9. Clearing,
993), Felim Egan.

131. Tabarca,
(1994), Sean Scully.

132. The Taking of Christ *by Caravaggio (1571–1610). Missing for centuries, the painting was discovered in Dublin in 1992. It has been fully restored by the National Gallery of Ireland, where it is now exhibited.*

■ *Funding and Development*

Since the introduction of bursaries and studio grants in the 1970s and the development of galleries and arts centres, a structure has been provided within which the visual arts can flourish. Businesses are developing collections and sponsoring exhibitions and events and municipal authorities are allocating budgets for the arts. The 'Aosdána' scheme, which is administered by the Arts Council, provides for a collegiate of 200 creative artists and for five-year annuities to those wishing to work full-time at their art.

During the past decade, the Arts Council has paid particular attention to developing access to the arts in those parts of the country outside of the major cities. Central to this process was the creation of arts centres

where the public could have access to theatre, music and the visual arts. The Council supports centres in Wexford, Waterford, Cork, Tralee, Listowel, Mullingar, Limerick, Galway, Castlebar, Sligo, Monaghan, Drogheda and Dublin (three). Twenty of the country's 33 major local authorities employ specialist Arts Officers who organise and promote theatre, music and the visual arts. The Arts Council and the Arts Council of Northern Ireland co-operate closely on joint projects such as touring. To accommodate the growth in sculpture, there are two art foundries in Dublin and the National Sculpture Factory (1989) in Cork.

Reflecting the upsurge of interest in the contemporary visual arts, the Government established a new *Museum of Modern Art* at the Royal Hospital, Kilmainham. With the addition of the completed *RHA Gallagher Gallery* in Dublin the capital is now well-provided with large, well-equipped public exhibition places.

The standing of the arts and culture was enhanced with the establishment in 1993 of a new *Department of Arts, Culture and the Gaeltacht.*

Major development of the national cultural institutions is underway, including the conversion of Collins Barracks, near the centre of Dublin, for use by the *National Museum.* The *National Library* is to be extended and its services improved, and development is continuing at the *National Gallery.* Proposals are being developed to relocate the *Chester Beatty Library*, with its prestigious collection of Islamic, Oriental and Christian manuscripts, paintings and other works of art, to the Clock Tower at Dublin Castle.

Cultural relations abroad are assisted through the Advisory Committee on Cultural Relations ('the Cultural Relations Committee') which advises the Minister for Foreign Affairs on expenditure on projects involving Irish artists outside Ireland.

■ *Ancient*

The earliest examples of Irish architecture still visible today are the megalithic tombs. Dating from the Neolithic period (3700–2000 BC) these great tombs are built of large stones and vary considerably in size and shape. The dolmen is a simple form of tomb, with three or more standing stones supporting one or two capstones: the capstones can be up to 6 metres long. The court-cairn, a rectangular burial chamber built of large stones and usually covered by a mound, represented a more complicated form of tomb.

A more developed megalithic tomb is the passage-grave. Passage-graves consist of one or two burial chambers covered by a large earthen mound, with access through a passage from the edge of the mound. These tombs date from around 3000 BC. The best-

Architecture

133. The ecclesiastical buildings on the Rock of Cashel, Co. Tipperary include Cormac's chapel, a fine example of Irish Romanesque architecture.

known examples, Newgrange (see page 18), Knowth and Dowth, are located in close proximity to each other in the valley of the River Boyne near Drogheda. At Newgrange the mound is almost 11 metres high and 85 metres in diameter and the passage is about 19 metres long. The roof is constructed by corbelling, placing layers of flat stones one on top of the other, each layer protruding inwards over the one below. The passage-graves are the work of a well-organised and advanced civilisation. At Newgrange a small opening in the stonework is so designed as to admit sunlight to illuminate the central point of the burial chamber on 21 December, the shortest day in the year. Unlike other megalithic tombs, some of the stones in passage-graves were ornamented with geometric designs.

During the Bronze Age (2000–500 BC) smaller megalithic tombs appeared: these had burial chambers surrounded by stones on three sides and were covered by a wedge-shaped mound. However, most Bronze Age tombs were simple stone-lined compartments for individual burials.

The construction of large fortifications probably dates from the Iron Age (after 500 BC). Large circular stone forts were built, often on hilltops. One of the most impressive monuments of this period is Dún Aengus on the Aran Islands, a huge semi-circular stone fortress built right at the edge of high cliffs with strong defensive protection. Smaller ringforts, constructed of stone or earth, probably served as fortified dwellings. Another type of dwelling, the *crannóg*, was an artificial island of stone and wood constructed in the middle of a lake.

■ *Early Christian and Medieval Period*
No wooden churches have survived from the early Christian period. On the rocky crag of Skellig Michael (see page 139) off the Kerry coast there is a group of oratories and beehive huts, all built according to the corbel technique, forming a primitive monastery. On the mainland in Co. Kerry, Gallarus Oratory is of a similar construction. While these buildings may be as late as the 12th century, their mode of construction still shows Stone Age influences. The earliest stone churches are small, simple structures, with little or no ornamentation. Very few of them date from before AD 900.

The Irish round tower is found in many parts of the country. These towers, built from the 10th to 12th centuries, are tall slender stone structures, tapering inwards at the top, with a conical roof. They are frequently more than 30 metres high. Round towers are found on monastic sites and their primary purpose seems to have been to serve as bell-towers. However, the raised level of the doorway indicates that they may also have had defensive uses.

The first examples of Romanesque architecture in Ireland date from the 12th century. Influenced by the highly decorated churches found elsewhere in Europe, this style of architecture reflects increasing contact with the outside world. The finest example is Cormac's Chapel on the Rock of Cashel in Co. Tipperary. Although Irish churches remained small in scale, they were renowned for the intricate sculpture found on the doorways and chancel arches. Much use is made of traditional motifs, such as interlace and animal patterns, both seen to full effect on the spectacular portal at

*Facing page:
134. Dún Aengus,
the Aran Islands.*

Clonfert cathedral.

The new monastic orders which arrived in the 12th and 13th centuries — Cistercians, Dominicans, Franciscans — had a major influence on architecture. They built larger cruciform churches with side aisles separated by arcades. Adjoining the church, the domestic buildings were grouped around a cloister.

From the arrival of the Anglo-Normans onwards Irish architecture was strongly influenced by England. Great new cathedrals in the early Gothic style were constructed by the Normans in the main towns. These were distinguished by the use of pointed arches. Among the finest examples are the two Dublin cathedrals, Christ Church and St Patrick's (see page 11), both completed in the first half of the 13th century.

The earliest fortifications built by the

Normans were earthen mounds with wooden fortifications on top. Within a short time they were building more substantial stone castles, such as those at Trim in Co. Meath and Carrickfergus in Co. Antrim, each having a massive rectangular keep. The 15th century castle at Cahir in Co. Tipperary, surrounded by high enclosing walls and defended by eight towers, is the most impressive of the surviving feudal strongholds.

The early 15th century saw the emergence of the tower house. This was a stone rectangular fortified residence of many storeys and there are hundreds of examples dotted around the countryside. A particularly elaborate example of the tower house is Bunratty Castle in Co. Clare, now completely restored. Tower houses continued to be built in great numbers throughout the 16th and early 17th centuries, a turbulent period in

135. The Casino, Marino, Dublin.

Irish history. There is also an impressive group of semi-fortified mansions, influenced by the architecture of Tudor England. Relatively few buildings of this period survive in Irish towns, but a well-preserved example is Rothe House in Kilkenny. It gives some idea of the fine merchants' houses which must have lined the city streets of the period: it is a three-storey stone building fronting on to the street, with arcades leading into courtyards. The house reflects the English urban architecture of the period.

■ Classical Period

Classical buildings do not appear in Ireland until the later 17th century. An early example (ruined) of a residence which is clearly a classical country house rather than a defensive castle is Eyrecourt, Co. Galway, of the 1660's. Beaulieu in Co. Louth is an excellent surviving example of a once common type of pre-Palladian Irish country house.

The first Classical public building was the Royal Hospital in Dublin. Designed by Sir William Robinson and built in 1680–84, it was a home for retired soldiers modelled on Les Invalides in Paris. The buildings are ranged around an arcaded courtyard, with the great hall and chapel on one side and the living quarters on the other three. The building is now completely restored.

Palladian architecture, inspired by the buildings and, more frequently, the publications of the sixteenth century Italian architect Andrea Palladio, first appeared in Ireland in the early 1700's. The largest and most palatial Palladian country house is Castletown in Co. Kildare. Designed by Alessandro Galilei and Sir Edward Lovett

Pearce, it was completed between 1722 and 1732: there is a central block, a Roman palazzo, linked to two service wings by curved colonnades of Ionic columns. The interior is noted for its elaborate plasterwork by the Francini brothers. Several other Palladian mansions were built in this period, many of them designed by the German Richard Castle.

Pearce was the most important Palladian architect of his day. His most famous building is the old Parliament House (now the Bank of Ireland) in Dublin's College Green. Designed in 1728, it has a piazza forecourt surrounded on three sides by Ionic colonnades and it is the earliest large-scale Palladian public building in the country. Castle was responsible for Leinster House (1745), designed as a town-house for the Dukes of Leinster, and now the seat of parliament, and for the Rotunda Hospital, which he designed in 1751.

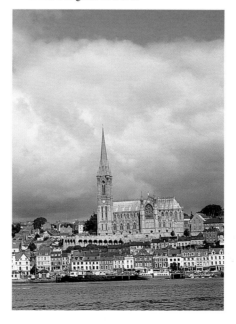

136. St Colman's Cathedral, Cobh.

At the end of the 18th century the Palladian style gave way to Neo-Classicism, looking directly to ancient Rome. The great architect of this period was James Gandon (1743–1823). Gandon designed some of the most beautiful public buildings in Dublin including the Custom House, begun in 1781, and the Four Courts (see page 55), begun in 1786. Both buildings present impressive columned riverside facades and each is topped with a magnificent dome. Francis Johnston (1760–1829), who designed the General Post Office in Dublin's O'Connell Street, completed in 1818, exemplified the growing self-confidence of national architects in the post-Gandon era.

■ *Modern Period*

The early 19th century saw the emergence of a native architectural profession and the Royal Institute of the Architects of Ireland was established in 1839. The first decades of the century witnessed a spate of building and much of the architecture of the period is characteristic of the international Neoclassicism then common in Europe and America. Good examples are Carlow Court House, by William Morrison, 1828, and the Church of Our Lady of Refuge, Dublin, by Patrick Byrne, 1850.

The revival of the Gothic style is usually associated with church-building and there are numerous churches of this type. They are distinguished by their tall, thin towers and pointed spires surrounded by smaller pinnacles, they are usually rectangular in plan with a square tower and they often have battlements. Among the finest examples of church architecture of the period are St Fin Barre's Cathedral in Cork, by William Burgess, 1867 and St Colman's Cathedral, Cobh, begun in 1868 by E.W. Pugin and G.C. Ashlin. The Gothic style was adopted for domestic architecture in the construction of Ashford Castle in Co. Mayo (c 1870), designed by J.F. Fuller.

In the late 19th century there was a brief Celtic revival in architecture associated with the Gaelic literary movement. A typical example is the Honan Chapel, Cork, by James F. McMullen, 1915. However, though the idea of a Celtic revival promised much, it had only a limited influence on Irish architecture.

The influence of the modern movement was first seen in domestic architecture and in small scale buildings generally. The first significant modern building was the terminal building, Dublin Airport, by Desmond FitzGerald, 1940. An important building of the post-war period was Busárus (the Store Street bus terminal), Dublin, by Michael Scott, 1953, who was one of the leading exponents of modern architecture in Ireland.

In the 1960's and 70's there was considerable expansion in architecture especially in the areas of factory building and educational buildings and churches. Factory buildings such as Carroll's, Dundalk (Ronald Tallon, Scott, Tallon, Walker, Architects 1970) shows the ability of Irish architects to provide the country with attractive industrial landscapes. Schools such as Birr School by Peter and Mary Doyle, 1980 combined new educational theories, rigorous discipline and native technology. In the area of church building, Liam McCormick is regarded as a most significant architect; a fine example of his work is the Church of St Aonghas at Burt, Co. Donegal.

Facing page:
137. The Carroll's factory, Dundalk.

138. Local Authority housing, Shannon.

139. School of Engineering, University College, Dublin.

140. Birr School.

141. Limerick City Offices.

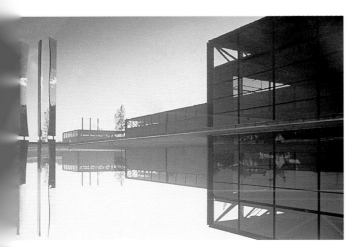

In the 1980s, during a period of reduced building activity, there was considerable debate among architects on the development of a new Irish architecture with greater concern for context, the environment and urbanism. The conservation of the country's built heritage became increasingly important with major projects such as the Royal Hospital, Kilmainham by John Costello of Costello Murray Beaumont, and subsequent conversion of the building into the Irish Museum of Modern Art; the restoration of the Custom House and Dublin Castle, by the Office of Public Works; and the Casino at Marino (see page 166), Dublin, by Austin Dunphy and John Redmill.

Local Authority housing showed a new concern for street pattern and context; the early 1980s saw the end of public deck/access apartment buildings. Schemes such as City Quay Housing, Dublin by Burke-Kennedy Doyle; Rutland Street by Dublin Corporation Architects Housing Department; and Share Housing, Cork by N. Hegarty, Cork City Architect, showed the influence of the street as a design determinant. New housing on a human scale, with clear definition of the public and private realms, was built.

Private housing also underwent radical change with innovative and elegant schemes for high density city housing being designed, such as Oak Apple Green by Denis Anderson. New standards in apartment design and imaginative interpretations of vernacular architecture were seen in such schemes as Mount Shannon Housing by Murray O'Laoire.

In the 1990s there was a new concentration on architecture and urbanism with the introduction of tax incentives for development in run-down areas in the major urban centres and towns. An example of an important urban initiative undertaken in the 1990s is Temple Bar, an area in Dublin which was the subject of a limited competition for an architectural framework plan. A wide range of new building types by a variety of architects is being built, providing a unique integration of new cultural uses, new urban spaces, housing and commercial development.

■ *Towns and Cities*
Ireland was outside the Roman Empire and excluded from one of the chief benefits of Roman civilisation: its towns and cities. As a result, the first urban settlements had their origins in Celtic society, and their immediate genesis in the form of the early Christian monastery. In the absence of a central authority these institutions acquired an important role in Irish life, and the first concentrations of people grew up in the shadow of large monasteries like Clonmacnoise in Co. Offaly and Glendalough in Co. Wicklow (see page 7). Huts and workshops accumulated around the circular enclosure with its churches and round tower forming the elements of an ecclesiastical city.

The earliest recognisably European towns, with streets, walls, and timber houses, were small Viking trading settlements built around the coast in the 9th and the 10th centuries. Wexford (see page 48), Waterford and Limerick were founded in this way, while Dublin, established in 841, grew to be a place of some importance in the affairs of Viking Europe.

The Norman colonists laid the foundations of a comprehensive urban network in Ireland. From the 12th century they were responsible for building and incorporating scores of small, fortified, trading towns in the south and east, many located along rivers or adjacent to feudal castles and abbeys. Kilkenny city, granted a charter in 1207, is a good example: it evolved as a disciplined rectangle of streets within a ring of stone walls, towers and gates. Laid out along the river Nore between the castle and the cathedral, it contained a parish church, several abbeys, and substantial merchants' houses on the main street. Youghal in Co. Cork gives some impression of the close density within the ramparts of a medieval town, narrow streets with gabled houses, towers and churches in close proximity to one another. Athenry in Co. Galway has significant remnants of its walls and Drogheda in Co. Louth retains its 13th century St Lawrence's Gate.

The reconquest and plantations of the 16th and early 17th centuries initiated a new era in Irish history and a new phase of formal town planning. The town of Bandon in Co. Cork, founded by the Earl of Cork in the early 17th century, has a Classical plan where regular plots of land stand on streets intersecting at a Market Square. Like Derry, its layout has references to the ideals of the Renaissance, and its plan has parallels in the colonial towns of North and South America. Castlefinn in Co. Donegal, one of many plantation villages built across the north, repeats the ideal on a more humble scale.

The 18th and early 19th centuries witnessed some of the greatest achievements of town planning in Ireland. Dublin became one of Europe's most beautiful capital cities, laid out with well-proportioned streets and squares of red-bricked Georgian houses embellished by magnificent public buildings. The elegance of Georgian Dublin can still be seen in Merrion and Fitzwilliam Squares.

Landlord towns were created in every part of the country, often set out as grandiose plans with their axis focused on a local monument, the church, the market house or

142. Georgian Dublin.

the gates of the local great house. Tyrrellspass in Co. Westmeath is planned as a semi-circle with the church at its highest point; Templemore in Co. Tipperary has its elongated town square with the town hall as its focal point. These towns and villages are universally built up with narrow three and four storey houses with brightly painted facades and, traditionally, with elaborate and decorative shopfronts.

Music and Dance

In common with most of the great art music of the world, the art music of medieval Gaelic Ireland was non-literate. The harp was the dominant and characteristic instrument in historical times, and was adopted as the arms of Ireland in the 17th century. Since the music of the old bardic system was not written down no record of it survives. One of the few early composers whose work has survived is the poet, harpist and composer, Turlough O'Carolan (1670–1738). Since his death, 220 of his works have been collected and published. Following the Belfast Harp Festival of 1792 Edward Bunting transcribed and published the traditional airs of the participants. This collection, together with the later collections of Petrie, Joyce, and others was the principal source of the airs adapted and made popular throughout Europe in the 19th century and afterwards.

The European art music tradition is also well represented in Ireland. In the 18th century Dublin became an important centre of music attracting such composers as Francesco Geminiani (1687–1762) who played and taught music in Dublin; Thomas Arne, the leading English composer of his day; and Handel who held the premiere of

143. Monument to Turlough O'Carolan, (Oisín Kelly), Mohill, Co. Leitrim.

the *Messiah* in the city in 1742. An Irishman with considerable influence on Romantic composers from Chopin to Glinka was John Field (1782–1837), creator of the nocturne and one of the foremost pianists of his day.

Two Irish-born composers of the 19th century who achieved distinction through their operas were Michael Balfe (1808–70), whose best-known composition was *The Bohemian Girl,* and Vincent Wallace (1812–65) who composed *Maritana.* Charles Villiers Stanford, born in Dublin in 1852, and who later became Professor of Music at Cambridge University and the Royal College of Music, London, was a prolific composer of operas, orchestral and choral music. Many of his compositions, such as *Irish Symphony* and *Six Irish Rhapsodies*, reflect his origins. Victor Herbert (1859–1924), principally known for his operatic compositions, and Hamilton Harty (1879–1941), whose most widely known work was his *Irish Symphony,*

144. *La Bohème by Leoncavallo at the Wexford Opera Festival.*

145. *Cork School of Music Big Band at the Guinness Cork Jazz Festival.*

based on folk songs, was also highly regarded. Brian Boydell (b. 1917) has written for both orchestra and for string quartet and his work has been mainly influenced by Bartok and Hindemith.

Composers A.J. Potter (1918–80), and Gerard Victory (1921–1995), through his links with the RTE Symphony Orchestra after 1967, have been major influential figures on the music scene in recent times. Other well-known composers are Seoirse Bodley (b. 1933) and John Buckley (b. 1951), and in the case of composers who have studied and established themselves abroad major figures are Frank Corcoran (b. 1944), Gerald Barry (b. 1952) and Raymond Deane (b. 1953). Within the past decade a number of composers have emerged who are experimenting with traditional music within an orchestral context. These include Shaun Davey, Mícheál Ó Súilleabháin and Bill Whelan.

One of the most striking features of the music scene this century has been the resurgence of interest in Irish traditional music. It was the advent of the *Fleadh Cheoil* (Music Festival) in the 1960's which unlocked the doors to allow the older rural-based traditions access to the streets and halls of the newly emerging urban Ireland.

The country's discovery of its own music went hand in hand with a period of economic growth and a consequent attitude of self-confidence. This culminated in the 1960's with the work of Seán O Riada (1931–71) who as well as engaging himself in orchestral composition (in a quasi-serial style) also created something of a musical revolution by forming a band of traditional musicians of the highest calibre, *Ceoltóirí Chualann*. While it is widely accepted that his original intention of creating a uniquely native art music fell short of his hopes, there is no denying the influence which his particular brand of traditional music had in other areas. The most notable example of this influence, and the most loyal to the O Riada model, is *The Chieftains* group, whose largely uncompromising concert arrangements of traditional music have brought them acclaim from audiences around the world.

A most fertile fusion of elements of acoustic-pop and traditional music took place in the 1970's. This resulted in a blend which was at once Irish (as represented by traditional musicians playing in authentic style on traditional instruments) and popular (as represented by musicians from more popular forms of music playing stringed, fretted instruments in accompaniment). Traditional instrumental music, therefore, enjoys great popularity in Ireland at the present time. The main national collection of materials relating to traditional music is housed in the Irish Traditional Music Archive in Dublin.

Traditional vocal music includes English and Scottish ballads imported centuries ago, and Anglo-Irish songs and ballads dating mostly from the 19th and early 20th centuries, which were popularised by Thomas Moore and Percy French. Above all, the form of singing Irish in the old style or *sean nós* must be mentioned. *Sean nós* is usually sung solo, and the music relies on the melody ornamented by melismatic, rhythmic and intervallic variation. A great number of *sean nós* songs have been collected by the Irish Folklore Commission (now the Department of Folklore at University College, Dublin). Traditional instrumental music is played on instruments such as uilleann pipes and includes dances such as jigs, reels, hornpipes, slides and polkas as well as slow airs based on the vocal music.

The two main varieties of popular music at the present time are 'country' music and the more cosmopolitan rock music. The growth of maturity in Irish rock bands since the seventies has seen rock music emerge as a natural expression for a growing number of

musicians. Some of the most widely known Irish rock artists of recent times have been U2, Van Morrison, Clannad, Enya, Sinéad O'Connor, Chris de Burgh, The Cranberries, Paul Brady and the Saw Doctors. The successes of Irish bands and writers internationally have brought growth to the music industry, currently valued at over IR£150 million p.a. and employing some 10,000 people. In 1988, the Arts Council appointed its first Popular Music Officer and the post led to the establishment in 1992 of Music Base, a national organisation which provides services to support the development of popular and rock music.

Radio Telefís Éireann is the backbone of professional music performance in Ireland. RTÉ maintains *the National Symphony Orchestra*, which has been the platform for the launching of most large-scale modern Irish compositions, and the *RTÉ Concert Orchestra*. Other orchestras include the *Irish Chamber Orchestra*, the *Cork Symphony Orchestra* and the *National Youth Orchestras*.

Dublin Grand Opera Society presents two seasons of opera in Dublin annually, principally of mainstream operatic repertoire from the 19th and 20th centuries. *Opera Theatre Company*, also based in Dublin, specialises in small scale touring productions which it brings to centres throughout the country. *Wexford Festival Opera*, a 15-day event at the end of October, has achieved a major international reputation. There are regular recitals organised in the premises of the Royal Dublin Society, the Royal Hospital, Kilmainham, and the National Concert Hall, each presenting eminent international ensembles and soloists, as well as Irish artists. Music societies in all of the major

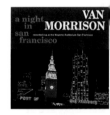

The Chieftains (146.) and U2 (147.) are perhaps Ireland's best known performers on the international stage.

regional cities present a season of concerts and recitals each year. Major music festivals which attract participants of many nationalities include the *Cork International Choral Festival*, the *Waterford Festival of Light Opera*, the *Kilkenny Arts Week*, and the *Guinness International Jazz Festival* (in Cork).

148. Performance at Siamsa Tíre, Tralee, Co. Kerry.

While there is no national ballet or dance company a number of small dance companies and dance organisations are active, particularly in the area of modern and contemporary dance. These receive State support through the current Arts Council Dance policy of providing financial assistance for public performances on a project basis. In the past number of years there has been an increased emphasis on youth dance and on dance-in-education. A professional dance-in-education company, *Daghdha*, is based at the University of Limerick. The national folk dance tradition is represented by the *Siamsa Tíre* company based in Tralee, Co. Kerry.

Irish cinema currently enjoys a higher international profile than ever before. Films such as *Ailsa* (dir. Paddy Breathnach 1994), *The Crying Game* (dir. Neil Jordan 1993), *The Snapper* (dir. Stephen Frears 1993), *The Commitments* (dir. Alan Parker 1990); and *In The Name of the Father*, *The Field*, and *My Left Foot* (dir. Jim Sheridan 1993, 1990 and 1989 respectively) have been box-office and critical successes throughout the world. There is a new focus on the increasingly attractive resources for production and on the wealth of film-making talent available. This is a most exciting and vigorous period of growth for Irish film.

The history of cinema in Ireland is a long and colourful one. Dublin had its first public screening of films from the Lumière brothers in April, 1896. In February, 1897 the first filmed Irish subjects were shown by Professor Jolly in Dublin. They included items such as *"People walking in Sackville Street, Traffic on Carlisle Bridge and the 13th Hussars Marching through the City"*. The first dedicated cinema, the Volta in Dublin's Mary Street, opened in 1909. James Joyce worked there at one stage. Fortunately, one could argue, he was no great success as a cinema manager, and tired of the venture after a short time.

In 1910 Ireland played host to the Kalem company, a touring film company from the United States. Under the direction of Sidney Olcott, Kalem made several short Irish

Cinema

melodramas in Co. Kerry and thereby launched a tradition of great film-makers using Ireland as a back-drop for their work. Notable examples include Alfred Hitchcock's film version of Sean O'Casey's *Juno and the Paycock* (1930); Robert Flaherty's epic documentary *Man of Aran* (1934); Carol Reed's *Odd Man Out*; Francis Ford Coppola's *Finian's Rainbow* (1968), David Lean's *Ryan's Daughter* (1970); Robert Altman's *Images* (1972) and the films of Irish-American John Huston *Moby Dick* (1956), *The Mackintosh Man* (1973) and *The Dead* (1987). Perhaps the best loved and most widely known 'Irish' films are those of John Ford who made a number of highly acclaimed feature films in and about Ireland: *The Informer* (1935), *The Plough and the Stars* (1936), *The Quiet Man* (1952), and *The Rising of the Moon* (1957). More recently Ron Howard's *Far and Away* (1992), John Sayles's *Secret of Roan Inish* (1994), and Mel Gibson's *Braveheart* (1994) have exploited the landscape to stunning effect.

Among indigenous film-makers the most important production company from the early days was perhaps the Film Company of Ireland. Established by James Mark Sullivan in 1916, the company made a number of short Irish theme films (all of which were destroyed during the Easter Rising), and the feature films *Knocknagow* (1917) and *Willy Reilly and his Colleen Bawn* (1920). These films and *Irish Destiny* (1926), a love story set against the War of Independence, are important surviving examples of Irish cinema in the silent era. *The Dawn* (1936), another War of Independence story made by enterprising garage owner Tom Cooper, was Ireland's first indigenous sound film.

149. The Quiet Man.

Throughout the 1940s and '50s the National Film Institute (the precursor of today's Film Institute of Ireland) played an important role in producing many Government sponsored "information" type films dealing with subjects such as health, savings, rural modernisation, agriculture, etc. Gael Linn, which promotes the use of the Irish language, was an active producer in the late '50s and early '60s. The *Amharc Éireann* newsreel series made by Colm O Laoghaire and Jim Mulkerns was the most successful and longest-running theatrical newsreel produced in Ireland. Two documentaries, *Mise Éire* (1959) and *Saoirse* (1960), directed by George Morrisson for Gael Linn, were the first feature length Irish language films and were remarkable in that they comprised, almost exclusively, actuality film and newsreel from the period between 1900 and 1922.

The establishment in 1961 of *Telefís Éireann*, the national television service, provided work for a growing number of technicians and a training ground for film makers. The 1970s saw the emergence of a group of independent film-makers who began to engage more critically with social, economic and political issues than before.

The establishment in 1981 and reestablishment in 1993 of the *Irish Film Board* facilitated independent film production. Home-grown images of Ireland are now being brought to international screens by Bob Quinn (*Caoíneadh Áirt Uí Laoíre* 1975, *Poitín* 1978, *Bishop's Story* 1994), Joe Comerford (*Traveller* 1982, *Reefer and The Model 1988, High Boot Benny* 1993), Pat Murphy (*Maeve* 1982, *Anne Devlin* 1984), Thaddeus O'Sullivan (*The Woman Who Married Clark Gable* 1985, *December Bride* 1990), Peter Ormrod (*Eat the Peach* 1986), Alan Gilsenan (*The Road to God Knows Where* 1988, *Prophet Songs* 1990, *Between Heaven and Woolworths* 1992), Cathal Black (*Pigs* 1984, *Korea* 1995), Neil Jordan (*Angel* 1982, *Mona Lisa* 1986) and Jim Sheridan (*The Field, The Miracle* 1990, *Into the West* 1992 and *My Left Foot*).

Each year in October, March and July, the Cork, Dublin and Galway film festivals provide a showcase for new Irish and international cinema. Throughout the year the Irish Film Centre, housed in the restored Society of Friends Meeting House in Dublin's Temple Bar, provides a permanent venue for film producers to show their work. The Centre is home to a number of film-related organisations dealing in production,

distribution and exhibition. These include the *Film Institute of Ireland*, the national organisation for the promotion of film, *Filmbase*, the Federation of Irish Film Societies, Media Desk and Espace Video Européen. The *Irish Film Archive* is charged with the preservation of the nation's substantial film heritage. An important area of the Archive's work is its coordination of festivals of Irish film abroad. With the help of the *Cultural Relations Committee* of the Department of Foreign Affairs, the Archive brings programmes of Irish films to foreign venues, thus sharing this valuable aspect of Irish culture with audiences abroad.

The Government has introduced measures to encourage the development of the film and television production industry. The measures apply equally to foreign and domestic investors and have led to a significant increase in film production. While the norm previously had been the making of 2 to 3 films per annum, 1993 saw a dramatic increase with some 12 films completed. In 1994 some 18 feature length films and 11 major TV drama series were commenced and completed. These ranged in size and theme from international blockbusters to many indigenous stories produced on a relatively

150. Braveheart.

151. The Old Curiosity Shop.

low budget. The film studios at **Ardmore**, Co. Wicklow have entered a period of sustained activity with such projects as *The Old Curiosity Shop, Scarlett* (the sequel to *Gone with the Wind*) and *Braveheart* filmed there in 1994.

Measures to Promote Foreign and Domestic Investment in Film

— *Tax relief*: investments by corporations of up to IR£1,050,000 over a three year period, and investments by private individuals of up to IR£25,000 pa, may qualify for tax relief. ;

— RTÉ, the national broadcasting service, is to establish closer links with the independent production sector. IR£6.5 million will be made available by RTÉ for programmes from the independent sector in 1995, rising in stages to IR£10 million in 1998, and to IR£12.5 million — or 20% of RTÉ's television expenditure — whichever is the greater, in 1999;

— a third national television service, for Irish language broadcasting, is to be established. The new service, Teilifís na Gaeilge, will involve the commissioning of some 500 hours of programmes from the independent sector yearly.

Folklore

From time immemorial, the poet or *file*, was a leading personage in Irish culture and was accorded very high social status. The poets specialised in praise and satire, and their verses were thought by many to contain mystical knowledge and to have magical effect. Being the leading representatives of the learned caste, they were professionals and enjoyed the lavish patronage of Gaelic, and later Norman-Gaelic, lords. The traditional poetry survived the démise of the Gaelic social order, it being — from the 17th century onwards — composed in the more popular stressed metres known as amhrán ('song'). Living among the ordinary people and themselves often reduced to penury, the later Gaelic poets made a significant contribution to the sense of style and accuracy of expression which remains a distinctive trait of the Irish language.

This native stream of lore has left a considerable heritage of mythic and historical stories in contemporary Irish folklore. The adventures of the famous seer-warrior Fionn Mac Cumhaill are still known to, and related by, many Irish people. These include how he gained his wisdom as a boy by tasting the 'salmon of knowledge', how he triumphed over miscellaneous giants and magicians, and how he had the truths of life explained to him in a strange allegorical house. The champion Lugh, originally a god of the Continental Celts, is also remembered — especially how he slew his tyrant-grandfather who had a horrific eye which destroyed all on which it gazed. The adventures of the super-warrior Cú Chulainn are spoken of and tales are also told of more true to life characters, such as the quasi-historical High-King Cormac Mac Airt and the historical though much romanticised Conall Gulban, son of the great king Niall and contemporary of St Patrick.

Much lore centres on the patron-saints of

the various localities. These saints, historical personages from the early centuries of Irish Christianity, are portrayed in legend as miracle-workers who used their sacred power to banish monsters, cure illnesses, and provide food for the people in time of need. Holy wells, dedicated to individual saints, are still frequented on their feastdays in many areas, and people pray at these wells for relief from different kinds of physical and mental distress. Most celebrated were the national saint, Patrick; the great founder of monasteries, Colm Cille; and the ubiquitous Brighid who, as protectress of farming and livestock, preserves many of the attributes of the ancient earth-goddess.

152. Oisín and Niamh on horseback (Eamonn Costelloe).

Ireland is famous for its fairy-lore , which also contains vestiges of pre-Christian tradition. The fairies are known in Irish as the people of the sí, a word which originally designated a mound or tumulus, and the Irish fairies can be connected with early Celtic beliefs of how the dead live on as a dazzling community in their burial chambers. Through their identification in the medieval literature with the *Tuatha Dé Danann* ('People of the Goddess Danu') they may also be connected directly to the early pantheon of Celtic deities. In folk belief thousands of 'raths' — ancient earthenwork structures which dot the landscape — are claimed to be inhabited still be the sí-people, and many stories are told of humans being brought into these hidden palaces at night as guests at wondrous banquets.

Versions of numerous far-flung international folktales have been current in Ireland for many centuries. The simplest of these are fanciful little tales concerning the fauna, which deal with such matters as the fox and wolf, or the eagle and wren, pitting their wits against each other. Most popular of all are the 'wonder tales', which are long and lend themselves to very imaginative events and to highly stylised descriptions, and are therefore very suitable to storytelling in the Irish language. The plots of these stories are situated in a never-never land 'long ago', and they introduce the audience to impoverished young men on magical steeds who win the hands of beautiful princesses, to the overthrow of wizards and giants and dragons, and to many other kinds of wondrous and phantastic happenings. Of almost equal popularity are the 'novelle'-type tales based on other international plots concerning tricks and coincidences, but in a more true to life setting — many of these have, in fact, come to be told of leading Irish social figures such as Jonathan Swift and Daniel O'Connell. There is, of course, a large variety of humorous stories in Ireland, of both native and foreign derivation.

Respect for the dead has always been a prominent feature of Irish culture. Indeed, a very special female spirit, the *bean sí* is often heard to announce by her wailing the impending death of a member of a family. A wide range of beliefs and practices were concerned with the issues of death and burial and, in former times, the waking of the dead was an important social occasion. People not only prayed, but also sang, told stories, and even played games at the wake of a departed relative or friend who had enjoyed a long and fulfilling life. This was considered the proper way to pay tribute to the deceased person. Although this tradition of wakes has now all but disappeared, the more inherently joyful stages in the life cycle, such as births and marriages, maintain their age-old importance as great communal occasions and are celebrated with feasting and conviviality.

The compositions of the early poets were sung or chanted to the accompaniment of the harp, and there are several indications that occasional songs, working-songs, and laments were cultivated by the ordinary people with simpler patters of rhythm and metre. In the later Middle Ages, colourful love-motifs gained currency, particularly of the type which attributes the sympathy of the natural environment to human emotions. It is clear that these motifs were borrowed from Continental troubadour poetry, through the medium of the French and English languages. They were soon assimilated into native verse-forms to produce the many plaintive and touching love-songs which are still very popular in Irish.

Songs in Irish focus on the expression of feeling and rarely tell a story, and because of this the tradition of singing was influenced but little by the rapid spread of narrative ballads through other European countries in the post-medieval period. Such ballads were, however, introduced from England and Scotland in the course of the 18th and 19th centuries. They were often printed on broadsheets and sold at fairs and other gatherings, and thus formed the basis of Irish folklore in the English language.

Popular Irish songs were, and to an extent still are, sung without accompaniment, but music has long had an established context of its own. The earliest instruments were the harp and pipes, but in recent centuries violins and accordions were adopted and gained great vogue. The major division in Irish folk music is between melodious slow airs and lively dance-music. This latter is based on popular dances from England and Scotland, as well as on fashionable quadrilles taught by dance-masters who travelled the countryside. The populace developed the steps to their own more robust and vivacious taste, thereby giving rise to the traditional Irish set-dances which were performed outdoors in the summer and autumn, and in the dwelling-house when the weather was more inclement.

In the days before TV and commercialised entertainment, the most popular indoor pastime, apart from storytelling, was card-playing, to which many people were quite addicted. There was also a great taste for posing and solving riddles, for tongue-twisters, divination games, and of course for practical jokes. The indigenous festivals of the Irish calendar — such as St Brighid's Feast (February 1), May Eve, the festival of Lughnasa (August), and Halloween, all had their own special forms of amusements and preserved vestiges of earlier rituals. Of the Christian festivals, most custom centred on Christmas, Easter, St

John's Night, and the Feast of St Martin.

The realm of folk-belief is well represented in Irish traditional culture, and provides a good illustration of how realistic knowledge, derived from observation and experience, combines with fanciful ideas which are born of curiosity and lively imagination. In Ireland, as elsewhere, popular lore testifies to the fusion of the practical and the poetic. The life experience, the passing of time, the home and community, the different trades and skills, the natural environment, all have their own special beliefs attaching to them.

The Irish Folklore Commission was established in 1935, and has down through the years collected a vast amount of lore and ethnological data. It now functions as the Department of Irish Folklore at University College Dublin.

Sport

Ireland's role in world sport has in recent years been disproportionate to the size of the population. In team sports, The Republic of Ireland football team qualified for the World Cup Finals in 1990 and 1994. In individual sports many Irish sportsmen and women enjoy international stature. They include Darren Clarke in golf, Pat Eddery and Michael Kinane in horseracing, John Ledingham in equestrian sports, Steve Collins and Michael Carruth in boxing, Niall O'Toole in rowing, Ken O'Doherty in snooker, Michelle Smith in swimming and Sonia O'Sullivan and Catherina McKiernan in athletics. Stephen Roche and Seán Kelly have excelled in cycling.

The most widely played sports, however, are not international sports. The sports with the greatest following are Gaelic football and

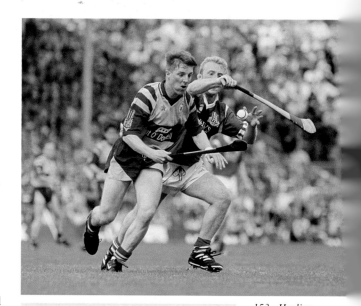

153. *Hurling*

154. *Gaelic football*

155. Soccer: Ireland
v Latvia.

156. Horse racing.

157. Michelle Smith.

hurling, and these are played almost exclusively in Ireland.

Many sports are organised on an all-Ireland basis and the performance of sportsmen and women from both parts of the island are followed with great interest throughout the country.

■ Gaelic Games

Hurling, Gaelic football and camogie are amateur sports, administered by An Cumann Lúthchleas Gael, the *Gaelic Athletic Association* or GAA, which was established in 1884 to promote and develop national sports. Gaelic football is a high scoring and exceptionally exciting field game, similar to rugby or soccer except that the ball is round and can be played with the hands. There are fifteen players on each team and scores can be either points, with the ball going between the posts and over the bar, or goals with the ball going under the bar. One goal is equivalent to three points. Hurling can be played on the same field as Gaelic Football and the rules are almost the same. The main difference is that hurling is played with stick and ball. It is recognised as one of the world's fastest sports. The major Gaelic competitions are the All-Ireland championships which are contested annually by teams representing each of the 32 counties. All-Ireland finals are played at Croke Park in Dublin, the country's largest sports stadium, and attract attendances of approximately 70,000 people.

■ Association Football

Association football, also known as soccer, is popular at all levels from schoolboy to senior. The major domestic competitions are the **National League of Ireland**, played in two divisions, a premier division of 12 teams and a first division of 10 teams, and the **Football Association of Ireland Cup**, a knock-out competition.

The senior domestic competitions, however, do not reflect the real strength of football. Like other small European countries Ireland does not offer adequate opportunities to its best footballers in domestic competition. Consequently many travel abroad to play, mostly to Britain. Under the management of Jack Charlton, the Irish international team has enjoyed great success and popularity.

Football in Northern Ireland is administered by the **Northern Ireland Football Association**, which fields its own international team and which has also enjoyed considerable success in international competitions.

■ *Rugby Football*

Ireland is one of a limited number of countries where rugby is a popular amateur sport. There is an extensive system of competitions at schoolboy, junior and senior levels organised on a regional basis in the four provinces — Leinster, Munster, Connacht and Ulster — and also covering the whole country. The principal competitions are the All-Ireland League, the Provincial Cups and the Inter-Provincials. Rugby attracts its biggest attendances to international matches. The **Irish Rugby Football Union**, the governing body for the sport, fields a team in the annual international championship contested by Ireland, England, Wales, Scotland and France. It also plays in the World Cup

Competition. Series of test matches are played on an occasional basis against Australia, New Zealand and other countries.

158. Rugby

■ *Athletics*

The long tradition of track and field athletics is reflected in the many medals won in the early Olympic competitions and the number of world records set by Irish athletes. Olympic champions include Dr. Pat O'Callaghan, Bob Tisdall and Ronnie Delany.

159. Sonia O'Sullivan.

There has been a significant increase in the numbers taking part in athletics in recent years, particularly running. Marathon races such as the annual *Dublin City Marathon* can attract thousands of participants. Some notable achievements have been recorded by the present generation of athletes: John Treacy has twice been world cross-country champion and won the silver medal in the 1984 Olympic marathon, Eamonn Coughlan was world champion at 5,000 metres, Marcus O'Sullivan and Frank O'Meara have won world indoor titles at 1,500 metres and 3,000 metres. Catherina McKiernan is the European cross country champion and has won 4 silver medals in the World Cross Country Championships. Sonia O'Sullivan won the European 3,000 metres championship in 1994.

■ *Equestrian Sports*

All forms of equestrian sport are popular. Horse-racing attracts large attendances at the many racetracks and there is a large business in off-course betting. Classic flat races are run at the Curragh; events such as the Irish Derby are among the most prestigious in Europe and the Irish bloodstock industry is considered one of the finest in the world. Hurdle racing and steeplechasing are also popular and Irish-bred horses are very much sought after by owners and trainers abroad. The main shows are the *Dublin Horse Show*, one of the premier events on the international circuit, the *Millstreet International Horse Show*, and *Punchestown International Horse Trials*. Eddie Macken, John Ledingham and Jessica Chesney are among the leading international showjumpers.

Ireland's open green spaces offer abundant opportunities for leisure riding. Riding stables are found in every county, many of them provide instruction and some offer residential holidays. Pony-trekking centres have been opened in many tourist centres in recent years.

■ *Golf*

More than 250 golf courses offer facilities throughout the country. Major competitions are organised on a provincial and national basis and all-Ireland teams compete in international amateur golfing competitions.

The major Irish tournament on the international professional circuit is the *Murphy's Irish Open*, one of the leading events on the tour. Irish golfers competing on the international circuit include Des Smyth, Ronan Rafferty, David Feherty, Philip Walton, Darren Clarke and Paul McGinley. The Dunhill World Cup was won by Irish teams in 1988 and 1990.

160. Killarney Golf Course.

161. Sailing in Killiney Bay, Co. Dublin.

■ *Boxing*

Olympic medals have been won by Fred Tiedt (silver), Freddie Gilroy and John Caldwell (bronze), Michael Carruth (gold) and Wayne McCullough (silver). World Professional Champions include Steve Collins, John Caldwell, Barry McGuigan, Dave McCauley and Eamon Loughran.

■ *Other Sports*

Ireland has over 3,000 miles of coastline and sailing is a long-established sport. The Royal Cork Yacht Club, founded in 1720, is the world's oldest sailing club.

A wide range of marine leisure activities are engaged in. These include fishing, sailing, waterskiing, surfing, canoeing, windsurfing, diving and cruising.

Other popular sports include greyhound racing, swimming, tennis, shooting and fishing.

IRELAND

Scale: 1:2 200 000

Miles in black / Kilometres in red	Belfast	Derry	Dublin	Cork	Galway	Kilkenny	Limerick	Waterford
Belfast		73 / 117	103 / 166	259 / 417	190 / 306	177 / 284	201 / 323	207 / 333
Derry	73 / 117		144 / 232	266 / 428	169 / 272	208 / 335	204 / 328	238 / 383
Dublin	103 / 166	144 / 232		158 / 254	132 / 212	71 / 114	120 / 193	101 / 163
Cork	259 / 417	266 / 428	158 / 254		130 / 209	92 / 148	65 / 105	78 / 126
Galway	190 / 306	169 / 272	132 / 212	130 / 209		107 / 172	65 / 105	137 / 220
Kilkenny	177 / 284	208 / 335	71 / 114	92 / 148	107 / 172		70 / 113	30 / 48
Limerick	201 / 323	204 / 328	120 / 193	65 / 105	65 / 105	70 / 113		80 / 129
Waterford	207 / 333	238 / 383	101 / 163	78 / 126	137 / 220	30 / 48	80 / 129	
Armagh	37 / 60	68 / 109	80 / 129	238 / 383	147 / 237	164 / 264	173 / 278	185 / 298
Athlone	141 / 227	130 / 209	79 / 127	136 / 219	58 / 93	72 / 116	75 / 121	102 / 164
Ballymena	28 / 45	51 / 82	121 / 195	296 / 476	209 / 336	192 / 309	231 / 372	222 / 357
Bangor	13 / 21	86 / 138	116 / 187	272 / 438	203 / 327	190 / 306	214 / 344	220 / 354
Bantry	319 / 513	336 / 541	215 / 346	56 / 90	182 / 293	151 / 243	117 / 188	134 / 216
Cavan	82 / 132	94 / 151	71 / 114	188 / 302	110 / 177	109 / 175	127 / 204	139 / 224
Coleraine	54 / 87	31 / 50	147 / 237	299 / 418	201 / 323	215 / 346	235 / 378	245 / 394
Donegal	112 / 180	43 / 69	145 / 233	250 / 402	127 / 204	192 / 309	184 / 296	222 / 357
Ennis	210 / 338	213 / 343	143 / 230	85 / 137	42 / 67	93 / 150	23 / 37	103 / 166
Enniskillen	86 / 138	61 / 98	109 / 175	224 / 360	114 / 183	144 / 232	163 / 262	174 / 280
Killarney	271 / 436	274 / 441	189 / 304	54 / 87	120 / 193	123 / 198	69 / 111	120 / 193
Larne	21 / 34	71 / 114	128 / 204	280 / 451	205 / 330	198 / 319	222 / 357	228 / 367
Letterkenny	93 / 150	20 / 32	147 / 237	279 / 449	156 / 251	207 / 333	218 / 351	237 / 381
Longford	114 / 183	114 / 183	79 / 127	163 / 262	69 / 111	97 / 156	102 / 164	127 / 204
Monaghan	54 / 87	67 / 108	78 / 125	216 / 348	138 / 222	137 / 220	155 / 249	167 / 269
Mullingar	110 / 177	132 / 212	54 / 87	152 / 245	87 / 140	73 / 118	93 / 150	102 / 164
Navan	85 / 137	125 / 201	30 / 48	171 / 275	105 / 169	91 / 146	121 / 195	121 / 195
Newry	38 / 61	87 / 140	65 / 105	218 / 351	164 / 264	136 / 219	165 / 265	166 / 267
Omagh	73 / 117	34 / 55	108 / 174	251 / 404	141 / 227	171 / 275	190 / 306	200 / 322
Portlaoise	156 / 251	175 / 282	53 / 85	109 / 175	94 / 151	32 / 51	71 / 114	62 / 100
Roscommon	139 / 224	131 / 211	97 / 156	156 / 251	50 / 80	98 / 158	93 / 149	129 / 208
Rosslare	205 / 330	247 / 397	95 / 153	129 / 208	170 / 274	61 / 98	131 / 211	49 / 79
Sligo	128 / 206	84 / 135	133 / 214	209 / 336	86 / 138	152 / 245	145 / 233	182 / 293
Tipperary	215 / 346	215 / 346	110 / 177	64 / 103	90 / 145	47 / 76	25 / 40	51 / 82
Tralee	264 / 425	267 / 430	185 / 298	74 / 119	128 / 206	133 / 214	63 / 101	132 / 212
Westport	192 / 309	148 / 238	160 / 257	182 / 293	52 / 83	159 / 256	112 / 179	192 / 309
Wexford	192 / 309	235 / 378	84 / 135	116 / 187	157 / 253	50 / 80	118 / 190	38 / 61

Roads

Rep. of Ireland
- Motorway
- Nat. Primary
- Nat. Secondary
- Regional

N. Ireland
- Motorway
- Class A
- Class B

Rail

International Boundary

Height in Metres
0
300
600
1200

Airports
- International
- Domestic

© Government of Ireland 1995

Ireland 1961–93: main economic indicators
*Annual % change**

	1961-73	1974-84	1985	1986	1987	1988	1989	1990	1991	1992[1]	1993[1]
Gross domestic product											
– At current prices	11.8	17.8	8.4	6.1	7.4	7.9	11.5	6.6	3.8	5.9	4.5
– At constant prices	4.4	3.8	3.1	-0.4	5.0	4.9	6.5	8.3	2.5	2.9	2.1
Share of gross fixed capital formation in GDP[2]	21.2	25.9	19.0	18.0	16.4	16.3	17.7	18.6	17.1	16.8	16.7
Inflation (price deflator private consumption)	6.3	14.5	5.0	4.6	2.9	2.5	3.7	1.7	3.2	2.9	2.2
Compensation per employee											
– Nominal	11.3	17.4	8.9	5.3	5.3	6.1	6.2	4.4	4.4	6.3	5.9
– Real (deflator private consumption)	4.7	2.5	3.7	0.7	2.4	3.5	2.4	2.6	1.1	3.3	3.6
– Real (deflator GDP)	3.9	3.5	3.5	-1.2	2.9	3.1	1.4	6.0	3.1	3.3	3.4
Productivity[3]	4.3	3.5	5.4	-0.6	5.1	3.9	6.6	4.8	2.6	2.8	2.0
Real unit labour costs[4]											
– Index: 1961-73=100	100.0	100.2	94.3	93.7	91.8	91.1	86.7	87.7	88.2	88.5	89.8
– Annual percentage change	-0.4	0.0	-1.8	-0.6	-2.1	-0.7	-4.8	1.2	0.5	0.4	1.4
Relative unit labour costs in common currency (against 19 competitors)											
– Index: 1961-73=100	100.0	95.6	97.8	103.8	98.6	96.3	91.0	90.6	86.3	88.7	93.3
– Annual percentage change	0.4	-0.4	0.7	6.1	-5.0	-2.4	-5.4	-0.4	-4.8	2.8	5.1
Employment	0.1	0.3	-2.2	0.2	-0.1	1.0	-0.1	3.3	-0.1	0.1	0.1
Unemployment rate[5]	–	10.3	18.2	18.2	18.0	17.3	15.7	14.5	16.2	17.8	19.2
Current balance[6]	-2.5	-8.4	-3.9	-2.9	1.2	1.5	0.8	1.3	6.0	6.7	6.6
Net lending (+) or net borrowing (-) of general government[6]	-3.8	-10.9	-11.2	-11.1	-8.9	-4.8	-1.8	-2.5	-2.1•	-2.7	-3.0
Gross debt of general government[6]	–	76.0	107.9	119.9	120.6	118.2	108.0	101.6	100.9	99.0	98.7
Interest payments by general government[6]	–	6.6	10.3	9.7	9.6	8.9	8.1	8.2	8.0	7.2	7.2
Money supply (end of year)[7]	12.1	16.6	5.3	-1.0	10.9	6.3	5.0	15.4	3.1	–	–
Long-term interest rate[8]	–	14.7	12.7	11.1	11.3	9.4	9.0	10.1	9.2	9.1	–

*Unless otherwise indicated.
1. Forecast.
2. At current prices.
3. GDP at constant market prices per person employed.
4. Deflator GDP.
5. Percentage of civilian labour force.
6. Percentage of GDP.
7. M3.
8. Levels.

Sources: Eurostat; EC Commission

These statistics are reproduced courtesy of the Institute of Public Administration, Dublin

POPULATION ━━━━━━━━━━━━━

Population: Republic of Ireland 1986–91

By counties and county boroughs

Province, County or County Borough	1986	1991			Change in Population 1986-1991	
	Persons	Persons	Males	Females	Actual	Percentage
TOTAL	**3,540,643**	**3,523,401**	**1,752,389**	**1,771,012**	**-17,242**	**-0.5**
LEINSTER	**1,852,649**	**1,860,037**	**913,617**	**946,420**	**7,388**	**0.4**
Carlow	40,988	40,946	20,786	20,160	-42	-0.1
Dublin Co. and Co. Borough	1,021,449	1,024,429	492,094	532,335	2,980	0.3
*Dublin Co. Borough**	*502,749*	*477,675*	*225,532*	*252,143*	*-25,074*	*-5.0*
*Dublin – Belgard**	*199,546*	*208,666*	*102,769*	*105,897*	*9,120*	*4.6*
*Dublin – Fingal**	*138,479*	*152,726*	*75,325*	*77,401*	*14,247*	*10.3*
*Dún Laoghaire – Rathdown**	*180,675*	*185,362*	*88,468*	*96,894*	*4,687*	*2.6*
Kildare	116,247	122,516	62,160	60,356	6,269	5.4
Kilkenny	73,186	73,613	37,449	36,164	427	0.6
Laois	53,284	52,325	26,910	25,415	-959	-1.8
Longford	31,496	30,293	15,523	14,770	-1,203	-3.8
Louth	91,810	90,707	44,792	45,915	-1,103	-1.2
Meath	103,881	105,540	53,510	52,030	1,659	1.6
Offaly	59,835	58,448	29,876	28,572	-1,387	-2.3
Westmeath	63,379	61,882	31,018	30,864	-1,497	-2.4
Wexford	102,552	102,045	51,425	50,620	-507	-0.5
Wicklow	94,542	97,293	48,074	49,219	2,751	2.9
MUNSTER	**1,020,577**	**1,008,443**	**506,570**	**501,873**	**-12,134**	**-1.2**
Clare	91,344	90,826	46,322	44,504	-518	-0.6
Cork Co. and Co. Borough	412,735	409,814	204,340	205,474	-2,921	-0.7
Cork Co. Borough	*133,271*	*127,024*	*61,260*	*65,764*	*-6,247*	*-4.7*
Cork	*279,464*	*282,790*	*143,080*	*139,710*	*3,326*	*1.2*
Kerry	124,159	121,719	61,792	59,927	-2,440	-2.0
Limerick Co. and Co. Borough	164,569	161,856	81,077	80,779	-2,713	-1.6
Limerick Co. Borough	*56,279*	*52,040*	*25,309*	*26,731*	*-4,239*	*-7.5*
Limerick	*108,290*	*109,816*	*55,768*	*54,048*	*1,526*	*1.4*
Tipperary, N.R.	59,522	57,829	29,352	28,477	-1,693	-2.8
Tipperary, S.R.	77,097	74,791	37,970	36,821	-2,306	-3.0
Waterford Co. and Co. Borough	91,151	91,608	45,717	45,891	457	0.5
Waterford Co. Borough	*39,529*	*40,345*	*19,721*	*20,624*	*816*	*2.1*
Waterford	*51,622*	*51,263*	*25,996*	*25,267*	*-359*	*-0.7*
CONNACHT	**431,409**	**422,909**	**213,989**	**208,920**	**-8,500**	**-2.0**
Galway Co. and Co. Borough	178,552	180,304	90,919	89,385	1,752	1.0
*Galway Co. Borough**	*47,104*	*50,842*	*24,282*	*26,560*	*3,738*	*7.9*
*Galway**	*131,448*	*129,462*	*66,637*	*62,825*	*-1,986*	*-1.5*
Leitrim	27,035	25,297	13,190	12,107	-1,738	-6.4
Mayo	115,184	110,696	55,963	54,733	-4,488	-3.9
Roscommon	54,592	51,876	26,687	25,189	-2,716	-5.0
Sligo	56,046	54,736	27,230	27,506	-1,310	-2.3
ULSTER (part of)	**236,008**	**232,012**	**118,213**	**113,799**	**-3,996**	**-1.7**
Cavan	53,965	52,756	27,307	25,449	-1,209	-2.2
Donegal	129,664	127,994	64,734	63,260	-1,670	-1.3
Monaghan	52,379	51,262	26,172	25,090	-1,117	-2.1

* As defined in the Local Government (Reorganisation) Act, 1985
Source: CSO

Population: Overview 1926–91

Total population		Figures for the intercensal period as shown in last column						
Year	Persons	Marriages registered	Births registered	Deaths registered	Natural increase*	Change in population	Estimated net migration**	Intercensal period
1926	2,971,992	230,525	968,742	731,409	237,333	-167,696	-405,029	1911-26
1936	2,968,420	136,699	583,502	420,323	163,179	-3,572	-166,751	1926-36
1946	2,955,107	159,426	602,095	428,297	173,798	-13,313	-187,111	1936-46
1951	2,960,593	80,868	329,270	201,295	127,975	+5,486	-122,489	1946-51
1956	2,898,264	79,541	312,517	178,083	134,434	-62,329	-196,763	1951-56
1961	2,818,341	76,669	302,816	170,736	132,080	-79,923	-212,003	1956-61
1966	2,884,002	80,754	312,709	166,443	146,266	+65,661	-80,605	1961-66
1971	2,978,248	95,662	312,796	164,644	148,152	+94,246	-53,906	1966-71
1979	3,368,217	171,705	548,413	267,378	281,035	+389,969	+108,934	1971-79
1981	3,443,405	42,728	146,224	65,991	80,233	+75,188	-5,045	1979-81
1986	3,540,643	95,648	333,457	164,336	169,121	+97,238	-71,883	1981-86
1991	3,525,719	90,692	277,546	158,300	119,246	-14,924	-134,170	1986-91

* Birth minus deaths
** Inward less outward

Population: Natural increase and net migration 1980–93 (000)*

Year	Population at mid-April	Total increase	Natural increase Since mid-April of previous year	Net migration**
1980	3,401	33	41	-8
1981	3,443	42	40	2
1982	3,480	37	38	-1
1983	3,504	24	38	-14
1984	3,529	25	34	-9
1985	3,540	11	31	-20
1986	3,541	1	28	-27
1987	3,546	6	29	-23
1988	3,531	-16	26	-42
1989	3,510	-21	23	-44
1990	3,506	-4	19	-23
1991	3,526	20	22	-2
1992	3,549	23	21	2
1993	3,563	14	20	-6

* Figures rounded to nearest thousand
** A minus sign denotes net outward migration

NATIONAL ACCOUNTS ━━━━━━━━━━━━

National income: Ireland 1987–93

Expenditure on gross national product at current market prices (£m)

Description	1987	1988	1989	1990	1991	1992	1993[1]
Personal expenditure on consumers' goods and services	12,845.4	13,811.3	15,378.3	15,800.4	16,607.0	17,575	18,065
Net expenditure by public authorities on current goods and services	3,574.7	3,539.5	3,685.6	4,082.3	4,480.4	4,842	5,167
Gross domestic fixed capital formation	3,453.1	3,567.1	4,277.3	4,886.7	4,642.2	4,661	4,808
Value of physical changes in stocks	27.8	26.2	274.9	721.8	639.1	-79	-179
Exports of goods and services[2]	11,855.1	13,633.6	16,136.8	16,115.8	16,892.6	18,707	21,871
Less Imports of goods and services[2]	-10,681.3	-11,920.9	-14,359.5	-14,514.0	-15,072.1	-15,718	-17,442
Gross domestic product at current market prices	21,074.8	22,656.7	25,393.4	27,092.9	28,189.2	29,987	32,290
Net factor income from the rest of the world	-2,112.4	-2,661.8	-3,232.8	-3,131.3	-2,865.0	-3,295	-3,727
Gross national product at current market prices	18,962.5	19,994.9	22,160.6	23,961.6	25,324.2	26,693	28,563

[1] Preliminary.
[2] Excluding factor income flows.

Expenditure on gross national product at constant (1985) market prices (£m)

Description	1987	1988	1989	1990	1991	1992	1993[1]
Personal expenditure on consumers' goods and services	12,098.9	12,636.0	13,631.4	13,805.6	14,161.2	14,573	14,741
Net expenditure by public authorities on current goods and services	3,223.3	3,062.8	3,034.4	3,211.9	3,297.6	3,378	3,415
Gross domestic fixed capital formation	3,297.3	3,244.8	3,684.3	4,154.7	3,812.7	3,741	3,722
Value of physical changes in stocks	17.4	-14.8	245.6	721.4	641.5	-39	-177
Exports of goods and services[2]	12,592.3	13,707.6	15,115.1	16,455.0	17,312.8	19,600	21,490
Less Imports of goods and services[2]	-11,729.7	-12,304.9	-13,873.3	-14,639.1	-14,834.1	-15,639	-16,557
Gross domestic product at constant market prices	19,499.6	20,331.5	21,837.5	23,709.5	24,391.7	25,614	26,632
Net factor income from the rest of the world	-2,243.7	-2,676.2	-3,028.1	-3,197.2	-2,936.3	-3,452	-3,662
Gross national product at constant market prices	17,255.9	17,655.2	18,809.3	20,512.3	21,455.4	22,162	22,970

[1] Preliminary.
[2] Excluding factor income flows.
Sources: CSO; Department of Finance

Agriculture: summary statistics 1986–93

	Estimated value (£m)							
	1986	1987	1988	1989	1990	1991	1992	1993[1]
1. Gross agricultural output (including value of changes in stocks)	2,720.5	2,871.6	3,163.0	3,376.6	3,224.8	3,140.4	3,360.3	3,456.8
2. Inputs of materials and services	1,289.3	1,179.4	1,228.8	1,348.0	1,362.7	1,376.9	1,378.5	1,441.1
3. Gross agricultural product (line 1 *less* line 2)	1,431.2	1,692.2	1,934.2	2,028.6	1,862.1	1,763.6	1,981.8	2,015.7
4. Incoming arising from agriculture (line 3 *less* levies and depreciation plus subsidies)	1,265.3	1,517.7	1,787.7	1,875.6	1,854.6	1,698.7	1996.3	2,048.5
5. Income from self-employment and other trading income	1,141.1	1,387.6	1,645.3	1,725.6	1,696.2	1,541.7	1,830.2	1,881.4

[1] Preliminary.
Source: CSO

Industrial production 1985–93
Volume index (1985 = 100)

	1985	1986	1987	1988	1989	1990	1991	1992	1993
Non-metallic mineral products	100.0	98.3	92.9	94.0	111.1	116.5	109.5	113.8	109.8
Chemicals	100.0	99.7	104.0	120.7	144.8	149.0	181.5	212.9	234.0
Metals and engineering	100.0	105.3	126.0	153.7	178.1	189.8	184.3	205.7	218.4
(Office machinery and data processing equipment)	(100.0)	(117.4)	(158.2)	(210.9)	(234.1)	(247.6)	(222.3)	(265.7)	(280.6)
Food	100.0	104.0	117.4	123.5	126.2	130.9	136.5	149.1	156.7
Drink and tobacco	100.0	101.7	100.1	105.5	116.8	117.2	122.9	122.4	122.3
Textiles	100.0	99.0	102.1	106.3	111.1	119.1	119.0	125.5	128.4
Clothing, footwear and leather	100.0	97.4	98.6	91.7	87.0	87.9	77.2	73.6	68.8
Timber and wooden furniture	100.0	95.7	96.3	105.8	111.1	117.5	117.5	120.4	121.9
Paper and printing	100.0	106.8	116.8	127.7	137.4	139.4	151.1	165.1	176.6
Miscellaneous industries	100.0	106.1	110.3	113.2	120.6	129.2	127.5	133.1	130.2
Total manufacturing industries	100.0	102.9	113.6	127.6	142.5	149.2	153.9	169.6	178.8
Percentage change	4.8	2.9	10.4	12.3	11.7	4.7	3.2	10.2	5.4
Mining and quarrying (incl. turf)	100.0	108.8	117.3	94.7	123.0	116.5	107.0	98.6	114.6
Total transportable goods industries	100.0	103.1	113.7	126.5	141.8	148.2	152.4	167.3	176.7
Electricity, gas and water	100.0	95.1	93.2	96.2	101.4	108.1	116.0	120.4	127.1
All industries	100.0	102.1	111.4	123.2	137.5	143.8	148.4	162.2	171.3
Percentage change	3.4	2.1	9.1	10.6	11.6	4.6	3.2	9.3	5.6

Sources: CSO; Department of Finance

Gross National Investment 1987–93 (£m)

	1987	1988	1989	1990	1991	1992	1993*
Gross domestic physical capital formation	3,480.9	3,593.2	4,552.2	5,608.5	5,281.3	4,581	4,629
Net foreign investment	-59.7	62.2	-348.0	37.2	924.9	1,431	2,594
Gross national investment	3,421.1	3,655.4	4,204.2	5,645.7	6,206.2	6,013	7,223

* Preliminary
Source: CSO

Interest rates (%): end period 1985-94

		One month interbank rate	Associated Banks[1] overdraft rate	Mortgage rage[2]
1985		10.4	10.5	9.75
1986		13.7	13.5–14.0	12.50
1987		8.2	9.0	9.50
1988		7.9	8.0	8.25
1989		12.4	11.0	11.25–11.95
1990		11.1	10.5	11.00–11.70
1991		10.7	11.3	10.75–11.45
1992	(Quarter 1)	10.6	11.3–11.5	11.25–11.95
	(Quarter 2)	10.1	10.8–11.3	10.75–11.45
	(Quarter 3)	21.0	11.5–17.0	10.75–11.45
	(Quarter 4)	18.0	19.0	13.75–14.45
1993	(Quarter 1)	9.4	11.0–11.9	10.75–12.45
	(Quarter 2)	6.7	7.5–7.8	7.75–8.95
	(Quarter 3)	7.0	7.5–7.6	7.75–8.45
	(Quarter 4)	6.6	7.0–7.4	7.75–8.45
1994	(Quarter 1)	6.2	6.6–6.8	7.25–7.95
	(Quarter 2)	5.4	5.8–5.9	6.85–7.25

1. Rates shown for times prior to December 1991 are AAA category overdraft rates. From December 1991 the rates shown are representative of those charged to large commercial borrowers for short-term borrowings.
2. The representative mortgage rate above refers to building society annuity mortgage rates. The Central Bank now quotes a range of representative mortgage rates, rather than a single rate, as in the past.

Source: Central Bank of Ireland

Price index numbers and percentage changes 1985-92

(1985=100)

Year	Consumer prices (all items)	Wholesale prices (general index)	Agricultural output prices	Agricultural input prices	Export unit value	Import unit value	Terms of trade
1985	100.0	100.0	100.0	100.0	100.0	100.0	100.0
1986	103.8	97.8	99.5	96.2	92.7	88.9	104.3
1987	107.1	98.4	103.5	91.7	92.7	88.8	104.4
1988	109.4	102.4	114.4	94.2	99.3	94.6	105.0
1989	113.8	108.1	120.1	99.3	105.9	100.7	105.1
1990	117.7	105.1	106.5	99.5	95.9	95.7	100.2
1991	121.5	106.4	103.1	99.8	95.2	97.9	97.3
1992	125.1	107.3	113.3	100.2	92.6	95.9	96.6
Percentage changes							
1985	5.4	3.0	-2.7	1.4	2.8	2.4	0.4
1986	3.9	-2.2	-0.5	-3.8	-7.3	-11.1	4.3
1987	3.2	0.6	4.0	-4.7	0.0	-0.1	0.1
1988	2.1	4.1	10.5	2.7	7.1	6.5	0.6
1989	4.0	5.6	5.0	5.4	6.7	6.5	0.1
1990	3.4	-2.8	-11.3	0.2	-9.4	-5.0	-4.7
1991	3.2	1.2	-3.2	0.3	-0.7	2.3	-2.9
1992	3.0	0.8	3.0	0.2	-2.7	-2.0	-0.7

Sources: CSO; Department of Finance

Purchasing power of the £: 1922-93

Taking value as equivalent to 100p in various years (read vertically)

1922	100														
1935	121	100													
1945	64	53	100												
1955	46	38	72	100											
1965	33	27	51	71	100										
1975	14	11	21	30	41	100									
1985	4	3	6	9	12	29	100								
1986	4	3	6	8	12	28	96	100							
1987	4	3	6	8	11	27	93	97	100						
1988	4	3	6	8	11	27	91	95	98	100					
1989	3	3	5	8	11	25	88	91	94	96	100				
1990	3	3	5	7	10	25	85	88	91	93	97	100			
1991	3	3	5	7	10	24	82	86	88	90	94	97	100		
1992	3	3	5	7	10	23	80	83	86	87	91	94	97	100	
1993	3	3	5	7	9	23	79	82	84	86	90	93	96	99	100

Source: Central Bank of Ireland

MONETARY

Official external reserves (£m): 1982-94

	Gold	Special drawing rights	Reserve position in IMF	Official ECU	Foreign exchange	Total
December						
1982	68.4	54.3	38.8	125.7	1,306.8	1,594.0
1983	93.3	45.9	74.9	242.2	1,558.6	2,014.8
1984	88.3	69.8	83.0	147.2	1,712.9	2,101.2
1985	76.4	60.5	79.2	265.4	1,790.5	2,271.9
1986	75.3	71.7	87.8	223.4	1,747.0	2,205.3
1987	83.0	83.2	88.0	173.9	2,393.2	2,821.4
1988	75.3	90.1	91.1	286.3	2,618.2	3,161.0
1989	69.8	100.1	82.7	178.2	2,090.1	2,521.0
1990	61.4	110.6	65.8	217.2	2,436.7	2,841.7
1991	59.2	120.6	81.4	197.1	2,797.6	3,256.0
1992	50.3	55.0	120.7	171.4	1,715.4	2,112.8
1993	100.7	92.1	148.0	308.5	3,628.6	4,277.9
1994 (June)	98.4	94.4	148.5	297.6	3,838.2	4,477.1

Sources: CSO; Department of Finance

Exchange rates: units per Irish pound 1980-94*

		US dollar	Sterling	DM	ECU	Effective index
1980		2.06	0.89	3.73	1.48	74.0
1981		1.62	0.80	3.64	1.45	67.8
1982		1.42	0.81	3.45	1.45	67.4
1983		1.25	0.82	3.18	1.40	65.1
1984		1.09	0.81	3.08	1.38	62.3
1985		1.07	0.82	3.11	1.40	62.4
1986		1.34	0.91	2.91	1.37	66.7
1987		1.49	0.91	2.67	1.29	66.2
1988		1.52	0.86	2.67	1.29	65.1
1989		1.42	0.87	2.67	1.29	64.4
1990		1.66	0.93	2.67	1.30	68.3
1991		1.61	0.91	2.67	1.30	67.3
1992		1.71	0.97	2.66	1.31	69.5
1993		1.47	0.98	2.42	1.25	66.0
1994	(Q1)	1.43	0.96	2.46	1.27	65.5
	(Q2)	1.47	0.98	2.44	1.27	66.0

* Period Averages   **Sources:** CSO; Department of Finance

PUBLIC FINANCE

Government revenue 1987-94 (£m)

	Outturn 1987	Outturn 1988	Outturn 1989	Outturn 1990	Outturn 1991	Outturn 1992	Outturn 1993	Budget 1994
Current Government Revenue								
Customs and Excise	1,479	1,589	1,770	1,788	1,842	1,859	1,916	2,070
Value-added tax	1,585	1,805	1,943	1,979	2,010	2,177	2,332	2,547
Income tax	2,713	3,055	2,810	3,024	3,231	3,413	3,712	3,797
Corporation tax	257	334	303	474	593	739	952	1,019
Motor vehicle duties	139	140	148	161	184	216	238	241
Stamp duties	169	198	279	271	250	256	227	240
Other tax revenue	148	201	190	206	247	250	327*	543*
Total tax revenue	6,493	7,322	7,443	7,903	8,357	8,910	9,704	10,458
Non-tax revenue	658	368	313	366	419	450	436	388
Total	**7,151****	**7,690**	**7,756**	**8,269**	**8,776**	**9,360**	**10,140**	**10,846**

* Other tax revenue includes income levy receipts of £79m and £44m for 1993 and 1994 respectively, and also includes tax amnesty proceeds of £242m for 1994
** Includes £3m income levy

Sources: Department of Finance; Central Bank of Ireland

Public capital programme 1985-94

£ million, current prices

	1985	1986	1987	1988	1989	1990	1991	1992	1993 Provisional Outturn	1994 Estimate	% change 1994 over 1993
Sectoral Economic Investment											
Agriculture and Food	59	62	50	70	64	82	92	122	137	**147**	+8
Industry	285	297	284	261	326	345	360	374	340	**353**	+4
Tourism	12	9	9	11	18	41	49	61	52	**70**	+36
Fisheries	7	5	6	4	7	10	10	8	7	**10**	+43
Forestry	19	20	26	22	28	42	47	43	44	**81**	+63
Miscellaneous	1	1	1	2	2	–	–	–	–	–	–
Sub-total	*383*	*394*	*376*	*370*	*445*	*520*	*558*	*608*	*579*	*662*	*+14*
Productive Infrastructure											
Energy	241	195	137	135	109	130	163	256	355	275	-6
Transport	76	67	92	114	130	219	197	158	123	**193**	+57
Roads, Sanitary Services, etc.	232	237	218	194	239	271	292	316	433	**380**	-12
Telecommunications, RTE, Postal Service	160	139	140	148	173	182	168	167	192	**223**	+16
Sub-total	*709*	*638*	*587*	*591*	*651*	*802*	*820*	*897*	*1,103*	*1,072*	*-3*
Social Infrastructure											
Housing	393	386	372	202	136	122	124	143	190	**296**	+33
Education	94	99	93	61	54	67	62	73	81	**99**	+22
Hospitals	57	59	58	44	48	46	42	44	44	**63**	+43
Government Construction, etc.	59	71	79	67	57	96	81	77	85	**186**	+118
Sub-total	*603*	*615*	*602*	*374*	*295*	*331*	*309*	*337*	*402*	*645*	*+61*
Grand Total	**1,695**	**1,647**	**1,565**	**1,335**	**1,391**	**1,653**	**1,687**	**1,842**	**2,084**	**2,379**	**+14**

The Department of Foreign Affairs wishes to thank those organisations and individuals who assisted in the preparation of this book and, in particular, contributions from the following people: Professor Máirtin Ó Murchú, Professor Augustine Martin, Mr Theo Dorgan, Professor Mícheál Ó Súilleabháin, Mr Shane de Blacam, Mr John Graby, Professor Joe Lee, Dr Dáithí Ó hÓgáin, Ms Sunniva O'Flynn. The Department of Foreign Affairs wishes to express its appreciation to the following for illustrations used in this book:

1,74	© ERA Maptec
2,12,13,43,44,45, 92,143,160	Slide File
3,4,5,6,7,8,9,17,20,30,36, 40,48,60,114,133,135	Office of Public Works
10	Gillian Murphy
11,37, 136	Bord Fáilte Éireann
15,98,134,148	Shannon Development
16	Royal Irish Academy
18	Bord na Gaeilge
21,23,123	National Museum of Ireland
22,115	The Board of Trinity College Dublin
14,24,31,32,33,62,109,113	National Library of Ireland
25	Courtesy of the owner
26	His Grace the Duke of Westminster
27	City of Leeds Art Galleries
28,112,117,124,132	National Gallery of Ireland
29	The Mansell Collection, London
34	BBC Hulton Picture Library, London
35	Biblioteca Vaticana, Rome
38,39	Government of Ireland
41	Pat Maxwell © Rex Features
42,87,90,91	Central Bank of Ireland
46	Department of Health
47,65,66	Office of the European Commission, Dublin
49	An Garda Síochána
50,51	Department of Defence
52	Neptune Gallery, Dublin
53,55,58	The Irish Times
54	Pat Maxwell
56,57,61	Northern Ireland Tourist Board
59	White House Photographers
63	Barry Mason; National Committee for Development Education (formerly DESC)
64	UN Photo 188094/E.Debebe 1067L
67	Baldwin W Old, Avondale, Lusaka
69	Thierry Grillet-Fournié/Newswork Press; The Ireland Fund of France
70	The Irish Post, London
71	The American-Irish Historical Society, New York
72	de Kun, Washington DC
73	The Irish Echo, Sydney
75	top left: IDA-Ireland, top right: Connaught Electronics, bottom: Irish Trade Board — An Bord Tráchtála

76,80,82,88,89,94	IDA-Ireland
77	Irish Food Board — An Bord Bia
78	Photo Images Ltd
79	Donald Smith
81	TDI, Dublin
83	Irish Trade Board — An Bord Tráchtála
84	Tara Mines Ltd
85	Electricity Supply Board
86	Susie Martin, Cityside Studios, London
93	The Geological Survey of Ireland
95	Moya Nolan; Irish National Teachers' Organisation
96	ARC: Burke-Kennedy Doyle and Partners, arch.
97	National Microelectronics Research Centre, Cork
99	Stephen O'Brien
100,120	An Post
101	Telecom Éireann
102	Finbarr O'Connell, AIPPA
103,104,105	Córas Iompar Éireann
106	Stena Sealink
108,110	RTÉ
111	Mary King, art teacher, Oldtown, Co. Dublin
116,119	Bill Murphy Design
118	Abbey Theatre, Dublin
121	Colour Books, Dublin
122 (see below)*	Barry Mason; The Great Book of Ireland, Dublin Castle
125	Bank of Ireland
126	Antoinette Murphy
127	Brian King
128	Paddy Graham
129,130,131	Kerlin Gallery, Dublin
137,138,139,140,141	Royal Institute of Architects in Ireland
144	Wexford Opera Festival
145	Guinness Cork Jazz Festival
146	RCA
147	Peter Stone © Not Us Ltd
149	© The Connacht Tribune; Irish Film Archive
151	Old Curiosity Productions
152	Eamonn Costelloe
153,154,155,156,157,158	Sportsfile
161	Rick Tomlinson; The Royal Irish Yacht Club
Page 174	Photographer Gerard Mooney

* text of *da tagte es* (1989 version) by Samuel Beckett: *redeem the surrogate goodbyes / who have no more for the land / the sheet astream in your hand / and the glass unmisted above your eyes*

The following is intended to provide an introduction to the topics covered in Facts About Ireland. Many of the publications listed contain extensive information as to further source material.

Land and People

The Shell Guide to Reading the Irish Landscape, *by G.F. Mitchell, Dublin, Town House & Country House, 1986.*

The Climate of Ireland, *by P. K. Rohan, Dublin, Stationery Office, 1986.*

Heritage, A Visitor's Guide, *ed. Eilís Brennan, Dublin, The Stationery Office, 1990.*

Ireland's Bird Life, *ed. Matt Murphy and Susan Murphy, 1994, Sherkin Island Marine Station Publications.*

Atlas of Ireland, *ed. J. P. Haughton, Dublin, Royal Irish Academy, 1979.*

Census of Population of Ireland 1991, *3 vols., Dublin, Stationery Office, 1993 and 1994.*

The Course of Irish History, *ed. T. W. Moody and F. X. Martin, Cork, RTE in association with Mercier Press, 1994.*

The Making of Modern Ireland 1603–1921, *by J. C. Beckett, London, Faber, 1981.*

Ireland since the Famine, *by F. S. L. Lyons, London, Weidenfeld and Nicholson, 1971.*

The Irish State

The Irish Constitution, *J.M. Kelly, Butterworths, 1994 (3rd edition).*

Nealon's Guide to the 27th Dáil & Seanad, *Ted Nealon, Dublin, Gill and Macmillan, 1993.*

Ireland 1912–1985, Politics and Society, *J.J. Lee, Cambridge University Press, 1989.*

The Government and Politics of Ireland, *Basil Chubb, London, Longmans, 1992.*

Administration Yearbook & Diary, 1995, *Institute of Public Administration, Dublin, 1994.*

Northern Ireland

The Ulster Question 1603–1973, *by T. W. Moody, Cork, Mercier Press, 1974.*

A History of Ulster, *Jonathan Barden, Belfast, Blackstaff Press, 1992.*

Governing without Consensus, *by R. Rose, London, Faber and Faber, 1971.*

Northern Ireland: a political directory 1968–1993, *by W.D. Flackes & S. Elliott, Belfast, Blackstaff Press, 1994.*

In Search of a State, *Fionnuala O'Connor, Belfast, Blackstaff Press, 1993.*

The Provisional IRA, *Eamonn Mallie & Patrick Bishop, Heimemann Ltd. (1987).*

Visitors Guide to Northern Ireland, *London, Moorehead, 1995.*

Ireland in the World

The Tortuous Path: The Course of Ireland's Entry into the EEC, 1948–1993, *D.J. Maher, Dublin, Institute of Public Administration, 1986.*

Towards a Safer Europe — Small State Security Policies and the European Union: Implications for Ireland, *Patrick Keatinge, Dublin, Institute of European Affairs, 1995.*

Ireland's Official Development Assistance 1993, *Dublin, Department of Foreign Affairs, 1994.*

The American Irish, *W.V. Shannon, New York, Macmillan, 1963.*

The Economy

Ireland in the European Community: Performance, Prospects and Strategy, *National Economic and Social Council, Dublin, 1989.*

Ireland in Europe, A Shared Challenge: Economic Cooperation in the Island of Ireland in an Integrated Europe, *Government Stationery Office, Dublin, 1992.*

The Single European Market and the Irish Economy, *ed. A. Foley & M. Mulready, Dublin, Institute of Public Administration, 1990.*

Economic Perspectives for the Medium-Term, *Sara Cantillon, John Curtis and John Fitzgerald; Economic and Social Research Institute, Dublin, 1994.*

Medium-Term Review: 1994–2000, *Sara Cantillon, John Curtis and John Fitzgerald; Economic and Social Research Institute, Dublin, 1994.*

The Economy of Ireland: Policy and Performance (6th Edition), *ed. John O'Hagan; Irish Management Institute, Dublin, 1991.*

The Macroeconomy of Ireland (2nd Edition), *Anthony J. Leddin and Brendan W. Walsh; Gill and Macmillan, Dublin, 1992.*

A Strategy for Competitiveness, Growth and Employment, *Report no. 96, National Economic and Social Council, Dublin, Nov. 1993.*

Ireland Guide, *Dublin, Bord Fáilte Éireann, 1992.*

Services

Report on the National Education Convention, *National Education Convention, 1994.*

Making Knowledge Work For Us — *report of the Science, Technology and Innovation Advisory Council, Stationery Office, Dublin, 1995.*

The Health Services of Ireland, *B. Hensey, Dublin, Institute of Public Administration, 1990.*

Care, Crisis, Control: The Development of the Social Welfare System: Ireland, *Mel Cousins, Dublin, Round Hall, 1994.*

Culture

Ireland: Art into History, *ed. Kennedy and Gillespie; Dublin, Town House & Country House; 1994.*

Traditional Music in Ireland, *Tomás O Canainn, Ossian Publications, 1994.*

Bringing it all Back Home — The Influence of Irish Music, *Nuala O'Connor, BBC Books, 1991.*

Irish Composers, *ed. Eve O'Kelly, Contemporary Music Centre, 1994.*

Cultural Policy in Ireland, *Anne Kelly, UNESCO & Irish Museums Trust, 1989.*

Myth, Legend and Romance: An Encyclopedia of the Irish Folk Tradition, *Dáithí Ó hÓgáin, London, Prentice Hall, 1990.*

The Irish Literary Tradition, *S.E.C. Williams and P.K. Forde, University of Wales Press & Ford and Bailie, Mass. 1992.*

The Field Day Anthology of Irish Writing, *ed. Seamus Deane, Derry, Field Day Publications, 1991.*

An Crann Faoi Bhláth, *ed. Gabriel Fitzmaurice & Declan Kiberd, Wolfhound Press, 1991.*

The Penguin Book of Contemporary Irish Poetry, *ed. Peter Fallon & Derek Mahon, Penguin, 1990.*

Wildish Things, *ed. Ailbhe Smyth, Attic Press, 1989.*

Irish Cinema: an Illustrated History, *Brian McIlray, Dublin, Anna Livia Press, 1988.*

Sport in Ireland, Annual Report of the Sport Section, Department of Education.